A PORTRAIT OF
BOWIE

A Tribute to Bowie by his Artistic Collaborators & Contemporaries

A PORTRAIT OF
BOWIE

INTRODUCTION
& INTERVIEWS
BRIAN HIATT

Contents

List of artworks

Introduction

The book you're holding is full of brilliant visual portraits of David Bowie, capturing him and his preposterously high cheekbones at every stage of his life – which included far more distinct stages than most humans manage. But the image that might come closest to capturing Bowie in his world-changing totality is an abstract painting by Stephen Finer, built upon the very impossibility of nailing him down. In the portrait, Bowie's face splays kaleidoscopically outward, as if caught between phases, as if he's the Sixties folkie, the Seventies glam alien, the clean-cut Eighties hitmaker and more, all at once.

Bowie was the greatest British rock star – maybe the greatest rock star, period – in part because he so casually transcended rock stardom, wielding its inherent poses and absurdities as tools. He was, at heart, a fine artist who turned the creation – and repeated re-creation – of his identity into a medium with as much potency as his music. It's no coincidence that on one of his earliest and greatest albums, *Hunky Dory*, he placed, one after the other, equally reverent songs about Andy Warhol and Bob Dylan. Bowie understood that being a rock performer – especially a British one, who would always be aping American sounds, American accents – entailed a certain amount of affectation, of artificiality. One of his many strokes of genius was embracing and amplifying that dilemma.

In his very first record, a 45 recorded with his band the King Bees in 1964, when he was still a suburban kid named David Jones, he affects a bluesy shout, like John

A brief note on the image-fall within this book: the 40 portraits broadly follow a chronological order, but for aesthetic and editorial reasons the chronology has, on occasion, been altered.

Lennon singing "Money". He was a white British kid imitating a more famous white Brit, who was, in turn, imitating black American performers. And Bowie was great at it: he could've sustained an entire little career with just that one pose – not a few rock singers did little more than that.

But as Jones changed his name to David Bowie, studied mime, dabbled in theatre, he realized that if playing rock meant inventing a self, why limit oneself to just one? Why not become a cracked actor, refiguring yourself from song to song? Why not turn yourself into a rock 'n' roll alien with a snow-white tan, a jaded Thin White Duke, or a slightly different alien with reddish hair? Why not expand your very music past the bounds of rock, embracing Philly soul and chilly Berlin electronics? And why stop there?

Bowie treated every photo, every TV performance, as a creation in itself – not as a mere promotional adjunct to the music. He was the first to imagine that a rock concert could be a truly theatrical presentation; his 1974 *Diamond Dogs* tour, with its cityscape set and elaborate choreography, was a glimpse of the future. When the tour hit Detroit, Michigan, a teenage Madonna was in the audience, taking mental notes. From there, the entire idea of the modern pop spectacle took shape.

Bowie was also a supreme collaborator, who understood decades early that a pop musician could succeed by curating as much as creating – no wonder Kanye West was a fan. Bowie realized he could rework his sound by choosing musicians, letting them do what they did best and then moving on to the next group: the Spiders from Mars never could've made *Young Americans*. On that album, and on 1983's *Let's Dance*, Bowie embraced African–American sounds by simply getting the musicians he'd admired on other records to play for him – an organic version of sampling.

Some of Bowie's closest collaborators – including keyboardist Mike Garson, guitarists Earl Slick and Carlos Alomar, *Let's Dance* producer Nile Rodgers, bassist Gail Ann Dorsey, drummer Zachary Alford, album art designers George Underwood and Derek Boshier and choreographer Toni Basil – offer intimate oral histories of their time with Bowie in this book, as do musicians and artists inspired by him, from Debbie Harry to Cyndi Lauper.

Bowie wasn't always in control of it all, as much as it seemed that way, as much as he knew how he looked at every angle, how he sounded in every corner of his voice. But even while he was half-crazed on cocaine in the mid-Seventies – famously consuming only that drug, milk and peppers for months – he made some of his best albums, posed for his most unforgettable photos, did some acting.

Decades later, while battling cancer in the final months of his life, he managed to finish a surreal, lovely musical, *Lazarus*, and one of his finest albums, *Blackstar,* before promptly passing away, as if he had planned it all out – which wasn't quite the case.

When David Bowie died on 10th January 2016, our loss was nearly immeasurable. This book stands as one of the first attempts to take that measure; to turn and face the strangest change of all: the idea of a world without any more versions of David Bowie.

Brian Hiatt is a senior writer at *Rolling Stone* **magazine in the US.**

George Underwood

British artist George Underwood designed album-cover artwork for musicians in the 1960s and '70s, including T. Rex, Mott the Hoople, Procol Harum and, most famously, his lifelong friend, David Bowie. Having abandoned his own foray into music in his late teens, Underwood went on to become celebrated for his figurative oil paintings.

When David and I first met in Bromley, we were about nine years old and both enrolling for the Cub Scouts. He was definitely skinny, but good looking. Strangely enough, our conversation went straight into music. Skiffle was all the rage in those days – there was a Lonnie Donegan record that was popular. Skiffle was kind of an early version of punk in a sense – go and buy a guitar, and *you* could do it as well. That was the idea, that one day we could have a skiffle group. And David's enthusiasm was just bursting at the seams.

That was what I liked about him. He was very enthusiastic about everything that he wanted to get involved in. In those days, when I first met him, they were called fads. You'd go in and out of things that you liked, and suddenly you'd brush them to one side and get enthusiastic about something else. David was the master of that, really: he was very good at being eclectic and gathering things around him, and making himself an expert on everything he touched. He could become knowledgeable about any subject in a short space of time.

THE MAN WHO FELL TO EARTH – GEORGE UNDERWOOD (1975)
This image was used on the 1976 reissue of Walter Tevis's 1963 novel The Man Who Fell to Earth, *published by Pan. Following the King Bees – and despite the offer of a solo contract – George gave up music to focus on art. His studio (Main Artery) coloured the artwork for the covers of* Hunky Dory *and* The Rise and Fall of Ziggy Stardust and the Spiders from Mars.

When I say "fads", it wasn't just about music. It was haircuts and style and the way you looked, and all those sorts of things as well.

I remember David having a trip to the barber's and getting what was called a Kennedy cut. A JFK. David would come to school with this new haircut, and we'd all go, "Ooh! It's a Kennedy cut." David was very keen to make sure that everyone knew that he was on the ball, as it were: "Oh, is it? OK!" We used to spend hours at school in the gents – the toilets – combing our hair, trying different styles of haircuts and so on. We were as vain as you could be.

The first gig I went to was Buddy Holly and the Crickets – when I tell people that they say, "Blimey, you must be old." I was 11 years old then. I'm now 69. It was a good start. I was the singer in a band called the Konrads when I was at Bromley Tech. I think David, who was learning the saxophone at that time, was quite impressed when he heard us play.

Eventually, I told the Konrads that I had a friend who played sax and they asked me to bring him along to rehearsals. We played a few gigs together, and eventually, when I left the band, David took over as the singer and sax player.

The funny thing was, David wasn't the only future rock star hanging around – Peter Frampton's dad, Owen, was our school art teacher, and he asked me to teach Peter guitar. I taught Peter the chords of "Peggy Sue" and told him to keep practicing. Of course, he was a total natural, and a week later he was playing it better than me, and had his own band, the Little Ravens.

––––

PORTRAIT FOR PYE – CYRUS ANDREWS (1966)

David photographed by Cyrus Andrews in a portrait session in 1966 to promote his first single under the Bowie moniker. In September 1965, David had adopted the name "Bowie" to avoid confusion with the Broadway star and soon-to-be Monkee Davy Jones. The shots were taken for the record label Pye who released the single "Can't Help Thinking About Me" by David Bowie and the Lower Third.

DAVID AND GEORGE (1972)
David (wearing a Clockwork Orange *T-shirt) and George (adopting a different smoking angle) during Ziggy's tour of the US in 1972.*

What was great about Bromley Tech – the school we were at – was that it had a stairwell outside the art room, which had great acoustics. So when it was raining – they called it a "wet break", when you'd have to stay in because it's pouring with rain – I brought a guitar in, and we used to sit on the stairwell. A load of the other kids would come and listen as well, and David was a great harmonizer; we did a lot of Everly Brothers and Buddy Holly stuff, and that was the beginning of our little bands that we got together.

———

David and I used to walk up and down Bromley High Street trying to pull the birds, basically. When it came to chatting up girls, we used to have such a laugh. We'd put on American accents or do something crazy… I remember once we were chatting up these girls and said we'd "just flown in from America", in American accents; that we were backing singers for the Everly Brothers; that we were actually in the band. And these girls were wide-open-mouthed. And David was just brilliant at it, you know; when it came to putting on accents, or mimickry, or anything like that, he was a gem.

David and I would do a sort of Pete and Dud act, you know, and just ad lib all the time. I miss his humour as much as anything else; he really was an entertaining, funny man. I think he was always able to switch it on. It's about being relaxed in front of people, and that's what David was… Probably, as time went by, I could see in interviews he was sometimes uptight about certain things; could see he wasn't quite relaxed. With me he could be dull, you know? I didn't expect him to perform in front of me, so we could just be as we were, naturally, without any audience.

Anyway, there was this girl at school and she had a friend who wasn't so pretty, and David used to say, "I don't like yours." He was always fooling around. And I said, "No, no, no, that's yours, mate, I'm not having the other one." We were both keen on this girl, and I said to David, "How are we going to talk to her?" She seemed so

untouchable... And I said, "I've got an idea" – my fifteenth birthday was coming up – "why don't I have a party and invite her over? Then the best man'll win. But at least we can start talking to her." So the party started – I invited her – and then everyone was drunk by about eight o'clock, it was terrible; there was so much alcohol that people had brought. David was absolutely wrecked, I remember my mother going over to him and pulling him by the shoulder because he had his head down on the table. "Are you all right, David? Can I get you a coffee?" And he said, "Oh, fuck off," and I thought, Oh, Christ. I've never said that to my mum! He was totally out of it.

I managed to sort of make this date with the girl the following week at this youth club, but David told me she couldn't make it, which wasn't true. She was there waiting for me for an hour. It was a bastard thing to do, really. It was just out of order. I was fuming about that. I mean, I'd never even kissed the bloomin' girl. You know, it was crazy. I'm not a fighter by any stretch of the imagination, but I was furious. David had been bragging about how he'd been going out with this girl who I'd wanted to go out with, and then she didn't want to go out with me, telling a whole pack of lies, basically, to my mates. I told a friend what had happened and he said, "Blimey, if that was me, I'd go over there and smack him one." And I thought, well, perhaps I ought to. Perhaps that's what you're meant to do. I ended up doing it. It was a stupid thing to do.

It was only a week later, after I'd come back from my errand round I did every Saturday morning, my father said to me, "You never told me you punched David Jones in the eye." And I thought, aye-aye, what's going on here? I said, "I didn't think there was any need to tell you, Dad, why?" He said, "Oh, I've just had his father on the phone

---

FIRST ALBUM COVER SHOOT – DAVID WEDGBURY (1967)

This shot was taken by David Wedgbury, who was, at the time, an uncredited Decca photographer for the image on the reverse of David Bowie's eponymous first album. Although very similar, the image on the front cover of the album was credited to Gerald Fearnley. The record was released on 1st June, 1967... the same day the Beatles released Sgt. Pepper's Lonely Hearts Club Band.

R&B ROCKER – DAVID WEDGBURY (1964)

A 17-year-old "Davie" Jones in 1964 in promotional shots taken by David Wedgbury for the group the King Bees. Their first single (and Bowie's) "Liza Jane" was realeased on 5th June, 1964 and featured Bowie on vocals and sax as well as George Underwood on guitar. The single had little impact on the charts and Bowie left the group soon after to join the Manish Boys.

and he's been rushed to Moorfields Eye Hospital." Oh my God. The shit hit the fan, and I went and saw him in hospital and said how sorry I was and everything, and, God, that was difficult, I can tell you, that was a toughie. And trying to explain it to his father – that was painful. It's weird thinking back on that really. But, you know, I just hope it's not engraved on my tombstone.

We kind of glossed over that: "It's not worth it." We never saw the girl again. It was such a stupid thing to get worked up over. So I kind of had to live with that. David did say later that I did him a favour, because it gave him his unusual look. That's why his left eye looks like that, of course.

We used to email each other towards the end – and we were talking about getting old, and I said, "Every time I look in the mirror I see my dad." And he said, "That's funny, every time I look in the mirror, I see your dad as well." That was the sort of humour he had.

———

When we both left school, he went on to a little advertising agency, and I went on to art college. We'd meet up, he was always coming round my house; we were always playing music. And when he was at this agency, one of the guys who worked there was a jazz enthusiast, and he used to say to David, "Could you go round to Dobells record store and get me this record that I've ordered that's come in?" It was the very first time I heard Bob Dylan, in fact – *The Freewheelin' Bob Dylan*. Charlie Mingus, *Oh Yeah*, which had Roland Kirk on it. It was an amazing introduction to jazz and all sorts of other music that ended up being hugely important to both of us.

I was at Haddon Hall – David and Angie's home, a gothic-mansion apartment in Beckenham – when he first played "Suffragette City" to me on his 12-string, and he said, "Oh, I've just written this. What do you think?" There were quite a few of us there, it wasn't just me, and he was doing the chorus – "Suffragette City... ya ya ya" and I shouted out, "Wham bam, thank you ma'am". And he said, "Oh, we'll keep that in." It fitted perfectly. I can't really take the credit – it was only because of David that I knew about "Wham Bam Thank You Ma'am" in the first place – it was one of the songs on that Mingus album!

One of the records we were listening to was by John Lee Hooker. And I was saying to David, "It's a strange way he plays guitar. Try something similar." So we called ourselves the Hooker Brothers, and we did John Lee Hooker numbers and Muddy Waters stuff as well. We did an interval set at something called the Bromel Club, at the Bromley Court Hotel, in Bromley, when the band went off for an interval, and a lot of our mates would rally round and cheer us on. It was fascinating. It was a learning curve.

And course, David being David, he was into something else the next week. The band didn't last much longer than a few weeks... But then David said, "We've got to get a decent band together," and he advertised for a band in *Melody Maker* and found these three guys from Fulham, which was quite a long way from Bromley, but we used to go on the train and see them and rehearse. And that was the King Bees.

I was playing guitar and singing, David was singing with me; we were harmonizing together. You know, "Hoochie Coochie Man", "Got My Mojo Working". All the type of songs that all the beat bands were doing at that time. We weren't writing our own material at all. Apart from that "Liza Jane" thing that we recorded: David and I sat down in my mum and dad's house and managed to bash that out one afternoon. The King Bees were just one of many bands at that time doing R&B and blues and stuff.

——

Back when we were at school, in 1962, we went to see Little Richard, who was David's hero. (Buddy Holly was mine, I guess – I actually got his autograph.) And about eight or ten of us from school got a block of tickets, where we were about six rows back from the stage – fantastic seats. It was this amazing package tour – Sam Cooke was on the same bill. So we're watching the show, and Little Richard climbs on top of his white piano while he's singing. It was a fairly slow number as I remember. All of a sudden, he goes, "Ooh, argh", holding his heart. I was sitting right next to David – David looked and me and he said, "What's going on?" and I said, "I don't know." And Little Richard fell on to the floor from the top of his piano – that's quite a long drop; we thought, something's definitely happening here.

David was getting very agitated, and then the MC came on and said, "Is there a doctor in the house?" Then we noticed all the musicians were crowded all around him, and David said, "Oh, we're seeing history being made here." He was actually convinced that he was dying on stage, and what happened was, all the musicians went back to their instruments, and the microphone was lying right by Little Richard's hand on the floor, and he picked it up and went, "A wop bop..." etc. and did "Tutti Frutti". And that's when David starting learning about showmanship, that wonderful other thing – he saw rock 'n' roll could be a real performance. Amazing. Getting the audience to be so concentrated on you and then coming out with a number like that... It was just magic. And David cherished that moment for a long time. It was theatre.

We had people like Screaming Lord Sutch, who used to come on stage in a coffin... Which was great theatre, you know? And of course you've got lots of other bands who were doing theatrical things. We had Nero and the Gladiators, who used to dress up as

---

SPACE ODDITY – DAVID BEBBINGTON (1969)

Taken in August 1969 by David Bebbington, this shot shows a hirsute David in his "space suit" at his home Haddon Hall, Beckenham, South London. Bowie had released the single "Space Oddity" the month prior in the UK and it reached number 5 in the charts with the BBC using it as background music for its moonlanding broadcast. It was released in August in the US, but couldn't get higher than number 124. The following year the single won The Ivor Novello award for originality.

gladiators... But David wanted something more than that. I could see David wanted to mix up everything together, and that's what he did.

Nothing is completely original, to my mind. I think there's always a link to something that's been before, whether it be in art or music; you'll always be able to find some kind of tenuous link somewhere that these things spring from. But I don't think that's faking it. Artists are allowed to steal, but not to copy – that's the premise, I think. The thing about David is that when you look at the real deal, they're faking it as well.

———

The King Bees ended because David said to us, "Ah, I'm leaving." We didn't know at the time, but he'd been rehearsing with another band. "Oh." But of course, David was ambitious and competitive. Our band wasn't that great, and I could see he wasn't going to be standing still for too much longer. I was a bit upset, of course, that it had to happen like that, but the manager of the King Bees, Leslie Conn, took me to one side and said, "Don't worry, George, I've got an idea, [record producer] Mickie Most is looking for a solo artist." Mickie Most was a big deal then, but he'd only done groups like The Animals... He'd never done a solo artist. I was shitting myself because I had to go and sing in front of him, in this little office. So I went up there, a bit nervous, and halfway through the song he said, "Stop!" and I thought, Oh, I've blown it, but he said, "George, I'd like to record you." It's like winning *The X Factor*. I suddenly had a five-year recording contract with Mickie Most, just like a few weeks after David had quit the band. Well, you can imagine, David was not too pleased about that. He was a bit pissed off, actually, and he didn't talk to me for a while.

Basically I'd taken the shortcut... I hadn't paid my dues, really. As far as he was concerned, you've got to be on the road for three or four years before you get that. But, anyway, I was lucky. It wasn't for me, though. I realized I wasn't the right kind of person for that business. So I quit, went back to art college, finished my course, and then went on to be a designer and all the rest of it. If I'd been in that business I wouldn't be talking to you now. I'd have been a casualty. I probably wasn't very good at saying no. There are too many things out there to fuck you up, and I think I was probably going to go in that direction. In fact, I think I had a bit of a breakdown. I didn't want to do it any more.

David was just about getting there. This is just before he did "Space Oddity", but it was kind of leading up to his first hit. His father died, and then he got this award for "Space Oddity". And I think that was the beginning of his rise to stardom.

He's a difficult person to pigeon-hole. I think he was searching, as they say. Like we all are, in one sense or another. But he realized that he hadn't found his voice. As an artist you're not satisfied until you find exactly what fits you, and you feel comfortable with it. I think that he, as a songwriter, was learning his craft. He was still learning how to write songs.

———

I went to the American tour in 1972, and he offered for me to go to his Japan tour, and I said no. I'd only been married a year, and it wasn't exactly a good start to a marriage to go on a rock 'n' roll tour. So I said, "No, I'd better go back and do my art. Anyway," I said, "if I was going to come to Japan, what would I be doing?" And he said, "You could do backing vocals... ". No, no, no! My days with the music business were over by then, and I was ready to try and do some painting, basically, which is what I'm doing now.

David asked me if I could do, not a likeness of him so much, but a character called Ziggy Stardust that he wanted, maybe, to put on posters, etc. It had David Bowie written on it, but Ziggy Stardust was to be on there, as if it was a cartoon character. It wasn't actually intended to look like him. It was a generic version with David Bowie in mind... I can't explain it. One time they were talking about doing an animated cartoon. That was one thing that came up. It never happened. David had talked about the Ziggy character coming from various people; he mentioned Vince Taylor, who was a rock 'n' roller from the late-Fifties/Sixties: he was on TV here, a black-leather-dressed rocker, who went over to Paris.

Some years later, when Taylor had been forgotten about over here, we were hanging out, and suddenly someone told us, "Vince Taylor is in London!" We couldn't believe it, but then Vince Taylor himself, with his dyed-black hair, came into the Giaconda – this coffee shop in Denmark Street, in Tin Pan Alley, where all the musicians used to hang out – and said to everyone in there, in this pseudo-American accent, "I'm havin' a party, and you're all invited! And the party's gonna last for two weeks!" It was in Park Lane – a very expensive part of London – and he gave us the address, and, lo and behold, that night it was absolutely teeming with people. But, to cut a long story short, he was a bit bonkers. I think he'd taken a bit too many drugs or something. Everyone knew that he was a bit crazy; he had a gun holster and a gun, which I was a bit worried about!

Anyway, I went back to Bromley – I was living at home at the time – and a week went by and I thought, I wonder if that party's still going? He had said it would last two weeks... So I went back and, you wouldn't believe it, there were still people there, crashed out, running around all over the place. And then what happened was that David had an encounter with Vince, and I think he talked about UFOs or something. He was a dramatically broken, psychotic sort of chap, old Vince; I thought he was brain damaged or something.

But David sort of saw him as a tragic figure. And I think that was one of the seeds for Ziggy. That was how he envisaged Ziggy. Burning himself out. Rock 'n' roll suicide. I said to him, it's the bravest thing I've ever seen anyone do: go on stage dressed like that.

———

BOWIE IN BED – RAY STEVENSON (1969)
Photo taken at Foxgrove Road.
"My memory is that it was the morning after the moon-landing.
Mary Finnigan says it was another time."

I thought it would either make him or break him. I mean, in those days people had never seen anything quite like that before. When David went to the States he said, "Tonight the crowd were a bit quiet there." And I said, "No, they were just standing there or sitting there with their mouths open, not knowing what to do." They'd never seen anything like it. It was a total surprise. It was such a spectacular show. And I think that once he'd created this character, it was very difficult to take the mask off. It was sort of taking over from David.

———

I did an interview many years ago with someone, and they asked me: "What is it that makes David different from other people?" And I said, "Well, I ring him up and I say, 'Do you want to come to a party on Saturday?' and he'd say, 'No, no, I want to stay in and get things done.'" That's what David was like. He knew when to go out and knew when to stay in and get things done. And of course that turned up in a song, "Modern Love", later. I liked that. From my point of view, I was actually quite proud that I said that, and he used it.

Once I was trying to get hold of him to get his permission to use his face on *The Man who Fell to Earth* book cover, which I was doing. And I said, he'll definitely give me permission. But the publishers said, "We need to know from him definitely." David was in the States, and I managed to get a phone number from someone and I left on the answer machine: "I'm happy, hope you're happy, too; give us as ring..." And those words appeared in "Ashes to Ashes", which I was pleased with. He sings, "Got a message from the Action Man/I'm happy/Hope you're happy too." But I don't know if I'm the Action Man!

It was fascinating when I heard that song for the first time and saw its video. I thought, Bloody hell, all these references! I drew that Pierrot with the woman, for the back of the *Space Oddity* cover – and there it was again, in three dimensions. Everything that you see on that back cover, all my work there, was in service of David's ideas. The astronauts holding the rose – that was based on the Iwo Jima memorial in Washington, D.C., with the GIs holding up the flag. David said, "Like that, but with a rose!" It was all clever things like that. The meditating man is Chimi – a little Buddhist he met – that's him sitting cross-legged there. David just wanted me to interpret his ideas. He always had so many references. Like with *Blackstar* and his final videos, it was a little like he was saying: "This is my life. This is what I did."

———

I can't think of anyone else as evocative in his influence on other people as David. I think Mike Garson's the musician who really misses David; it was a great combination they had. He brought out the best in people; in collaborators. If I spent a few minutes with David, I'd want to go home and start painting. There's something very unusual about that. You don't get that from many people...

David was always a believer in the underdog, a backer of things that looked slightly different. Like with music he had all these outrageously obscure people that he liked. Like Legendary Stardust Cowboy. Just one example of someone who no one else paid the blindest bit of notice to... And David'd go, "Nah, listen! Listen! Listen! Listen!" With art he went for German Expressionism... Things to get your head round sometimes. Things that weren't always easy to look at. He loved the classics as well, the Italian Renaissance, but he'd really go for the person who committed suicide when they were 25 or only did 12 paintings in their life or something. Always someone who's a bit obscure or weird and wonderful. I quite often thought, Dave! You don't like that, do you? And he did.

I had a show in 2014, and I said to David, "Could you write something nice about me for the show so I can have it on the invitation or something?" And he said, "Ooh, that's going to be a bit difficult, George! When's the deadline?" And I said, "Well, soon as you can do it", and he came up with this:

It's uncanny how these images inhabit their own world so completely. George breathes an icy life-form into them. They do not move, they are at permanent attention, as though on parade – subjecting themselves to our scrutiny.

I've always loved George's work. I think he may well have unconsciously tipped me towards music. Sitting alongside him in art class convinced me (among others) that I would never achieve his fluidity of line, his sense of rightness in relation to his subject, whatever it was. I persuaded my dad to advance me the money for an alto sax instead.

Over the years, George has risen above even his extraordinary beginnings and in my opinion is now producing some of the best work of his long and fecund career.

Talk about gushing, eh? It almost brought a tear to my eye, reading it again now. He was so generous. He always wanted to help me if he could. Ultimately, you've got to do it on your own, though. Like his son. He didn't know what he wanted to do, and David didn't want to give him too much of a leg up because, well, you can't have everything on a plate, can you? It's no good. And he's done fantastically well on his own. Quite a long time he was in limbo; now he's one of the top directors.

———

David was a very well-read chap. He used to read everything that was above- and underground. So he would have knowledge of, you know, Jean-Paul Sartre or whoever. I think David always wanted to be someone else in a way. "Oh, I'd like to be a bit like that person, or a bit like that person…" If I could go back in time to our school days and tell him, "Not only are you going to be a musician but you're also going to be a cult," he'd go, "Yes! That's exactly what I want!" And I'm so pleased that it worked out like that.

He was aware of pretty much everything he was doing – and he knew some of it might not work. But come to think of that, the only thing that truly was unacceptable to the public was Tin Machine. That didn't seem to go down so well but I quite liked it, actually. I remember him saying at the time, "I just want to be a member of a band", rather than the man up front. He was quite happy to try it out and see what happened.

———

David did say to me once, after the '72 tour, you might not see me for a few years, but it doesn't matter, because nothing'll change between us. It was a lovely thing to say, because I knew he was going off on a journey that was going to take him off all over the place, all over the world, to great heights... I've been very successful at avoiding fame and fortune all my life. I think David liked my company because I wasn't in the business, and I could be quite honest with him. I could say things to him other people perhaps couldn't say, like you do with your best mate. There'll never be another guy like him. Ever. From my point of view he was the best.

From other people I've spoken to, I think they definitely thought he had this potential, but from my standpoint it's kind of different, because we were best buddies. I knew he was special. Anyway, I'll never have a friend like him again because he was the best mate I could be with. He was so infectious with whatever he was into; he was always an inspiration to me. He'd always get me off my arse to do something; make me want to start creating, because he had that infectious quality. It's difficult to explain.

I don't think anyone realized he'd go to the heights that he has, that he did. I don't think anyone could predict he was going to be *that* phenomenally successful... But he did have the willpower and strength of mind to persist in what he was doing, even though there were a few obstacles in the way in the early days, releasing records that didn't make it. The stardust was embedded in him, somewhere along the line.

I'm quite pleased I didn't get a goodbye email. I'm glad I didn't know he was ill, really, because I would just have been thinking about it all the time. He did me a favour by not letting me know. That's the way I look at it. Although we hadn't seen each other in a long time, he sent me a hamper every birthday from Fortnum & Mason, and in 2015 I took a little video of myself and my wife with the hamper and sent it to him. He sent me back one of the last emails I ever got from him, which just said, "Oh, that's lovely… Give my love to all".

THE KING BEES – DEZO HOFFMANN (1964)

*The King Bees were: clockwise from top left – Roger Bluck (lead guitar); David "Davie" Jones
(vocals and saxophone); George Underwood (guitar, vocals and harmonica);
Francis Howard (bass guitar); Robert "Bobby" Allen (drums).*

Dana Gillespie

An ingénue singer and actress in the 1960s, Dana Gillespie is now a blues singer. As a teenager she spent her time in London's club scene, where she met David Bowie, Marc Bolan and Donovan, among others. Bowie wrote the track "Andy Warhol" for her, and introduced her to his manager, Tony Defries.

I used to go down to the Marquee Club in Soho when I was 14 years old, and David played there. When he finished at the end of the night I was at the back of the club, brushing my then waist-length hair. I'd just been offered a contract by the manager of the Yardbirds, and I was sitting there wondering whether to take it or not. David took the brush out of my hand and carried on brushing and said, "Can I come home with you tonight?" And I said, "Yes."

I had a very big, rather good house right in the middle of London, and my parents were on the fourth floor and my bedroom was on the fifth floor, so I just took him home, and he spent the night. Then, in the morning, when I introduced him to my parents as we came down the stairs to go off to school, my father thought he was a girl because no boys had shoulder-length, Veronica-Lake-style hair in those days. It was quite funny when they realized.

I was at school, but, you know, life is meant to be out there and experimental, and I had

---

DAVID BOWIE AT OAKLEIGH ROAD – RAY STEVENSON (1969)
*"David and Angie picked me up at my mum's house on the way to Wolverhampton
(in a Fiat 500 with speakers strapped to the roof – dangerously windy on the motorway!).
My mum made burgers for the three of us and insisted that David ate the bigger one
because he was so skinny."*

BOWIE AND THE BUZZ (1966)

Backed by his band the Buzz, Bowie on stage at The Marquee Club, London in April 1966. From left to right: John "Hutch" Hutchinson (guitar); David Bowie (vocals, guitar and saxophone); John "Ego" Eager (drums); Derek "Dek" Fearnley (bass); Derrick "Chow" Boyes (keyboards).

extremely cool parents, and they both quite liked David. People in the music industry seemed to have different kinds of relationships than normal people in those days. I was kind of living in a bubble. It was a great time to be growing up in the business, all the guys that I hung out with in those days, whether Jeff Beck or Jimmy Page, or whoever, they were just regular guys. Well, not regular, but musicians, and the musicians' world was small.

I have such a clear memory of the first night I saw David perform. He came on stage wearing knee-length, suede, fringed-at-the-top boots, kind of pirate-y-looking trousers, a white baggy-sleeved shirt and a waistcoat; a slightly Sherwood Forest/Robin Hood look. Not *Men in Tights*, a serious version. But he looked really cool; very hot actually. And the band was called the King Bees. In those days there was a little café called the Giaconda café in Tin Pan Alley/Denmark Street – now there's a blue plaque about it. It was the street where all the music publishers were based, and I often used to sit in the Giaconda for long hours with David, drinking a cup of tea – which is what one did in those days – waiting for somebody to come in and shout, "Is anybody a bass player?" or "We need a backing singer."

They'd take us, whoever was there, and then you'd go into the basement studios and do whichever things you were required for. David came in one day when I was sitting in the café, and he said, "Come round the corner." We headed off to a record shop, which doesn't exist any more, into one of those tiny booths. He played me a single, "I Pity the Fool", and the B-side was "Take my Tip".

He always loved image. I used to go with him sometimes when he'd go shopping, when he had a bit of money on him. We'd go down to Carnaby Street, which was trendy and very in, in those days; now it's just full of tourists. But then you could go down there and get yourself some really unusual clothing, and he'd go and get a military jacket with gold epaulettes or something. He didn't just slob out in a pair of jeans or a T-shirt. Never. I mean, maybe a T-shirt at home, but he would never walk out of doors looking like an old slob. He was very image conscious from the very early days. So when I look back and think about the Yardbirds at the Marquee, they'd just got on with their blues – doing Howlin' Wolf stuff, or whatever – but David, he posed when he sang. His body had a pose to it. He was born to pose.

After I'd met him at the Marquee Club, he said, "Come and meet the parents." So I had to get on the train to go to the edge of London, where he lived with his parents, in a sort of small, terraced, working-class area. They pretty much sat in silence in their little front room. I come from a house where everyone chatted, and social intercourse was the norm – we exchanged ideas, etc. He was rather horrified when he stayed at mine: he'd never been in such a house. His parents went out, and I remember David saying, "Whatever it takes, I am going to get out of living like this." He really meant it. It was that hunger, I think, that's always been underneath him: "I'm going to get out." And he did.

———

We stayed really good friends. A lot of people said, "Were you 'dating' him?" Well, first of all that's an Americanism, and I've never been on a "date" in my life. He used to listen to my songs, I used to listen to his songs; he showed me the first chords to play on my first live TV show, a song called "Love is Strange". He used to come and pick me up from school and carry my ballet shoes home. I mean, I know musicians, when they're on the road, they've got millions of girlfriends; that's what every lead singer or every young musician should do, in order to improve the writing quality, for a start. So he had the odd girlfriend but not very often, not until he met Angie and then he said, "I think you should meet her."

He wrote this song called "Andy Warhol" for me, which I did on the *Weren't Born a Man* album. In fact, he's singing and playing guitar; you can hear him on his good old 12-string in the back. This must have been 1972, and in the end it was basically Mick Ronson who produced it, because he suddenly got too busy to finish the album, but he loved the version that Ronson did [recorded in 1971] so much that he did his own version on *Hunky Dory*.

But I do remember, a couple of years before that, he just rang me up one time and said, "Oh, I've just written a song, I think I want to play it to you," and he came round half an hour later, sat down and played "Space Oddity".

He was always great to me – of course he got me with the same manager, Tony Defries at MainMan, so we had four or five glorious years of fantastic lifestyle, just really good fun, in England and then later on in America. I used to go with him to all the functions that there would be at the TV studios, because he was pretty good at networking. He was able to use his charm on a lot of people. And through that I landed up with the management company I was originally with, and then eventually, in 1970, I think, he said, "Tony Defries is our man, let's go with him."

———

I don't think anybody in England ever thought that such galactic fame like David achieved could exist. We had Elvis, who was big over here, but English superstars? Well, there were pop groups – obviously the Beatles – but I'd been around at a lot of his recording sessions, we lived in each other's pockets for a long time; he was just my old pal who I'd known since I was a young teenager.

I had a basement flat in a big house in the centre of London, under Harrods in Knightsbridge, and he would come over in between, I suppose, seeing other girls, or doing gigs and things; he and little Marc Bolan would be sitting writing songs together on my little tape machine – or big tape machine, I should say, they were big in those days. Every musician in London used to hang out in my place, so I never looked on him as destined for superstardom. I used to spend a lot of time with him, and when he was married to Angie, in the place they lived in, they would be sitting around surrounded by stacks of paper and writing ideas; Angie would be out getting the clothes and the food for the band. They were all hanging out in a place called Haddon Hall.

I first realized the full impact of how damn good he was when I went to see him when he did the *Diamond Dogs* tour, which never came to England. I knew everyone in it, and I knew everything that had been leading up to it. But sitting there, in the front row, with Angie next me, and having been at the rehearsals, and then seeing it work, I realized how supertalented he was, because I was able to sit back and look at him from the perspective of an audience. But, you know, when you know someone so well you don't think of that – "Are they going to be mega-big"?

When I was 15, maybe, I went to see him do his mime thing, which he was taking an interest in. He'd met Lindsay Kemp, who was famous for going on stage and doing his shows on acid. I may be wrong, but David was not really into psychedelics – I don't think – he didn't really like to lose control. David played the part of Cloud in one of Kemp's productions, *Pierrot in Turquoise*.

So I knew that he was interested in other things. He and I were both out of work, and we went to audition for *Hair*. Neither of us got it. That was quite funny. I then went on to play the first Mary Magdalene here in *Jesus Christ Superstar*, and he and Angie came to the show and left in the interval; they hated the music. I was so pissed off he couldn't have just sat through to the end for a friend's sake!

I saw him through all these phases. For a time he – and a lot of people – were obsessed with Anthony Newley. There was a certain kind of weird hipness to it. Anthony Newley had done the most bizarre television series called *The Strange World of Gurney Slade*,

---

DAVID AT TRIDENT STUDIOS – ROLF ADLERCREUTZ (1970)
This shot by Rolf Adlercreutz shows David in May 1970 at the Trident Studios, Soho, London where he was recording the album The Man who Sold the World, *released in November of that year.*

a kind of abstract-weirdo thing, and only the weirdest of the weird watched it. I was glued to it. I think it was in black and white. I don't think it was actually his songs that turned David on; it was the fact that he did weird and wonderful things – he was not your regular person... But Tony Newley was quite big then, years before he married Joan Collins. And Newley came through with a completely innovative way of doing a TV series. But it was a big, big thing for David, *The Strange World of Gurney Slade*.

He just explored all kinds of things; that's why I got on well with him, because I was also always doing various things, going to dance classes... We weren't just going out and being kind-of singers, you had to present what you were doing in a slightly different way. I remember going with him to the first Glastonbury Festival. David and Angie were dressed in identical grey and white Oxford bags, he with long hair and she with short hair. And, I mean, everyone was on everything; the audience and the whole thing was very untogether. David was meant to be on at nine o'clock at night, and by four in the morning he still wasn't on, and they were about to give him another day, because he was now going on at five in the morning... So at the Pyramid Stage, the sun starts to come up, and everyone's wandering up and crawling out of tents in the mud and everything, and he's up on stage alone singing "The sun machine is coming down, and we're gonna have a party" and that was a pleasing moment. Not everyone got it, and not everyone was conscious at five o'clock in the morning, but he had a sense of theatre, even then.

David knew his career needed him to be in America for him to spread his wings and fly. If anyone is ever going to be really famous in this business, you have to move to America. All of us had to up sticks and move to New York. Which was cool. And a lot of fun. I mean, I saw him go through some very troubled times, wild times, he changed very much when he got to America, or had been there a few years...

He would have something like 80 concerts in an 80-city tour; at night when everyone else had gone to bed or to a hotel room, he'd be up all night for whatever reason, often just sitting in the back of his limo. Obviously having ideas and writing on scraps of paper.

All of a sudden kabuki Japanese theatre might come on the TV, and he gets absolutely mesmerized by it, which he then incorporated into his work. I think he eventually went to Japan to check it out. He was always open to new ideas, and I think going to America opened his whole lifestyle as well.

———

I've personally thought one should never, ever marry a musician. I know them far too well. All of them. I don't mind having a good time with them, but marry? His marriage to Angie fell to pieces at the same time as the collapse of MainMan, like a house of cards or something. I thought we all had a strong foundation. But I'd be flying to RCA in New York with David, and suddenly nobody spoke to anyone, the money dried up; the whole company collapsed. He and our manager, Tony Defries, were in litigation, and I was in the middle with another contract, which involved litigation, because I was under the same umbrella. The thing was a flipping nightmare actually. And I was just sad, because what to me had been like a family was suddenly no longer there. I can't really comment on the marriage. I think she was very good for him at a certain time in his life, but many men aren't meant to be with one woman for the whole of their life, and that was probably true for David, until he met Iman.

They've been playing so many of his songs on the radio since his passing, and hearing some of the early ones brought it back to me how many different styles he'd done and how creative he'd been. He played a lot of instruments, but his real talent was getting other musicians to play what he wanted to hear. He never stood still. I don't think Tin Machine was a particularly good choice... I always used to think he was much better at acting a part, in a way. He was a cracked actor, after all.

I take my hat off to him: he happily turned himself into an enigma. It was very much brought home to me when he had this exhibition at the huge Victoria & Albert Museum in London. I lived literally opposite the V&A, and every day I'd see people queuing for miles down the street to come and see this, and actually they asked me to come and give a talk at the auditorium, which I did, but only about the early years.

My last contact with him must have been 1980-something or other. For the last twenty years or so, I've run the Blues Festival on the island of Mustique. Just before that he bought this house there; he never much enjoyed it or lived there much, and then he sold it on, and our paths never really crossed after that. If we were in the same room, it was always, "Hey! How are you doing?" Those things don't change when you've known somebody so long. Those innocent years. But back then, we were all trying to aim for something. And they were kind-of innocent; we were all trying to aim for something. For me, my god has always been music, but his has been music and performance art. And I remember he absolutely flipped when he saw the Andy Warhol play *Pork*.

People wrote me emails the day after his death, about how devastating it was and how awful, and I actually said, well, yes, terrible for his wife and children. But, as an artist, he did so much great work that it's not terrible at all. He managed to do the ultimate musician's dream, which is to get an album out about three days before you die. How cool is that? And he released his last video, as well. He stage-managed his own life pretty amazingly.

DAVID AND DANA – MICHAEL STROUD (1971)

Two MainMan stars, David and Dana, pictured in a studio shot from May 1971. David had finished recording "Hunky Dory" at this time, which featured Andy Warhol – a song Dana would perform for BBC Radio the following month. David had already begun work on songs that would feature on Ziggy Stardust and Dana would also feature on the album, providing backing vocals on "It Ain't Easy."

Mike Garson

American pianist and composer Mike Garson studied with Bill Evans and Herbie Hancock. Despite his jazz roots, Garson is probably best known for his work with David Bowie, from the tail-end of the Ziggy Stardust *tour to* Reality. *He has played keyboards with Nine Inch Nails, Smashing Pumpkins and No Doubt.*

Bowie was the ultimate casting director; 90 per cent of everyone he chose to work with was brilliant in their area, so he didn't have to guide them – he knew they had it. He needed to talk about his vision, and he just let them plug it in, because he was a kind of chameleon. He'd pull all these parts together and place them into one. So he was the ultimate fusion artist.

When I wasn't with David for a while, I played fusion music for a lot of years with Stanley Clarke during the Jazz-fusion period in the late Seventies – we mixed classical and rock and pop and jazz and New Age stuff. I don't like that word, but I was a fusion artist myself, so I understood what David was trying to do.

David absorbed everything, and he was able to make it his own – yet, at the same time, nothing was his own, and he knew that and he didn't care. I suppose looking at it from a darker side of things, he stole from everyone, but he said that. On the plus side, he made it his own and it's fresh, so it's not, in actual fact, dishonest. Yes, he took from people, but so have I as a pianist: that's how art works.

ZIGGY JUMPSUIT – MICHAEL PUTLAND (1972)

David in his "Ziggy jumpsuit" at Haddon Hall in April, 1972. The quilted suit designed by David and cut by Freddie Burretti was worn by Bowie on the cover image of the Ziggy Stardust *album. Burretti designed a number of David's outfits during the Ziggy era, including the "ice-blue suit" worn in the "Life on Mars?" video*

We absorb from history and the people who came before us, as well as the ones like John Lennon, who would be a few years older and parallel to David. But John would maybe be the only person David respected more than himself, and he learned a lot from him. John taught him a lot: he told me this. So aside from having a great friendship, you could say John raised his consciousness level. And John got him to realize that he was looking for love from all these people in the wrong places; it had to come from within. That's pretty deep.

John himself had obviously come through that, because artists tend to crave being liked and admired. That could be your Achilles heel, because then those people out there could make or break you. But if you don't give a fuck, what's the difference?

So I think John made that breakthrough in David, and God knows how he did it, but those English guys can be extremely sarcastic and cutting to each other, and that's how they play the game.

I would see Brian Eno with David, and they'd dance it back and forth. They were smart – it's English humour, they're a little covert and they have their dry sense of humour and they kind of whip you into shape by throwing these digs, and you don't even realize they just smiled and stabbed you in the back. He did it with Brian a lot, and I'm sure John and him did it with each other. And they don't see it as unethical or dishonest or nasty or mean-spirited. As an American I see it that way sometimes, but from their reality that's how you play the game.

———

Annette Peacock's the one who got me the job with Bowie. She has an album called *I'm the One*. I played the piano on it. If you compare the title track, "I'm the One" with the *American Psycho* remix of David's song "Something in the Air", which I played on, you'll hear similar piano elements. Now no one would know he stole that from Annette, because you don't even know who Annette is. She was another Charlie Mingus for him,

JOHN AND DAVID (1975)

Lennon and Bowie – shown here at the Grammys in March 1975 where David presented Aretha Franklin her award for best R&B star – were introduced to one another by Elizabeth Taylor and got along famously. They collaborated on the writing of "Fame", which released in July of this year and became Bowie's first US number 1 hit.

or another Bruce Springsteen, or another Mick, or Jacques Brel or Kurt Weill, another Lou Reed. Another big influence.

I did an avant-garde album with Annette the three months before I met Bowie, when I had a rock band, and she used that rock band but she used my jazz skills and my avant-garde skills.

So David comes to America, doesn't have a piano player. He comes here, he liked her, meets her, because he was very determined to meet whoever he artistically thought was great. He said, "Would you go on tour with me as pianist?" She said, "I have my own career and I'm probably not good enough to handle it. This is the guy for you. Call Mike Garson." And then I got the call that night. For 20 years I thought it was her recording engineer that recommended me, and he never denied it. I found out the real truth some time in the early Nineties!

I would drive with David in the limo through the United States on the *Ziggy Stardust* tour while he was planning the *Aladdin Sane* album, in 1972. I would see his thoughts and how he was obsessed and fascinated with America, and something was rolling in his brain. I didn't know it at the time, but it was that album baking baking – and we were finished recording *Aladdin Sane* by January 1973.

I was the perfect person to play on the album because I was one of the only jazz musicians that wasn't stuck in being only a jazz musician. I grew up in Brooklyn, a true New Yorker, living through the Sixties at the height of jazz. And Bowie and I bonded over jazz – he played the saxophone, he loved Charlie Mingus and Stan Kenton.

HUNKY DORY – BRIAN WARD (1971)

From this 1971 shoot came the cover of the Hunky Dory *album. The shoot was influenced by a book of Marlene Dietrich photos that David had with him at the studio. He asked his friend George Underwood to hand-tint a sepia photograph and he, in turn, passed this to his colleague at Main Artery to airbrush the print. The same technique was used on the next album* The Rise and Fall of Ziggy Stardust and the Spiders from Mars.

DAVID AND MIKE – (1974)

Mike Garson was hired to play on the Ziggy Stardust tour of the US in September 1972. The group had been through three previous keyboardists, so the contract was only for an eight-week term. However, Garson would remain with Bowie until 1975 and would reunite in the 1990s and continue to work together through to the Reality *album in 2003. This shot was taken during the recording of* Young Americans *at Sigma Sound Studios, Philadelphia, Pennsylvania, US, August 1974.*

The jazz guys dissed me when I went with Bowie, because they thought I was dropping down when in some ways I thought I was actually going up.

One of my closest friends was a great sax player, Dave Liebman. He went off with Miles Davis and I went off with Bowie; we both went to the top of the chain, but he thought of me as a piece of shit for going with Bowie, that I'd put all this eight-hours-a-day work in for 20 years and now I'm playing rock 'n' roll. Well, that same sax player, who's still my buddy, he didn't get what I did till a few years ago when his daughter was 17, and she said, "Dad, what you do is nothing, you should hear Mike Garson on *Aladdin Sane* with David Bowie." So his daughter straightened him out, and he called me and said, "Oh, I get it now."

———

On the first *Ziggy* tour I had these silver-and-black platform-high shoes that looked great. David had a crazy tuxedo made up for me, but not a normal black tuxedo. It had satin and lace and it was grey with a gigantic grey flower on it, and it sort of had tails – it looked sophisticated. So it wasn't as wild as the rest of the band, but it fit who I was, and the rest was the Spiders from Mars look. He developed the whole thing. He was a genius. He's fashion, man.

Around September of 1972, I walked into RCA studios in Manhattan to audition, and these guys were dressed up to the hilt, like they were going on stage; they were just rehearsing in the studio! I come in, in jeans and a T-shirt, and I thought, Where the fuck am I?

I was conscious at the time of the Ziggy Stardust character but he never laid that on me; I knew I was always talking to David Bowie. Don't let anyone fool you; he knew exactly who he was. But that was a good thing to hide behind, and it worked.

When I was in the studio with him doing *Diamond Dogs*, most of the time it was just him and me. There weren't other musicians. He was playing guitar parts, I was playing piano, synthesizer, harpsichord. So it was a very personal album for him.

I mean, think about each album he did. Pure brilliance. Did I know it at the time? Not a clue. Did history teach me a lesson? Yeah. Did I take playing with him for granted? Yeah. Did I even look down upon it a little bit as a classical and jazz musician? Yeah. Do I regret that? Yeah. Do I get it now? Yeah.

There was a part of me, for sure, that recognized his genius. And I loved playing in the band. But let me tell you for sure, there was another part of me at the time that just thought, This is way below my gift and abilities.

———

People always ask me, "What did he say?", but most of our working communication was kind of telepathic. What I do remember is David gave me a whole lecture on William Burroughs and how he inspired him to use cut-ups for the lyrics on *Diamond Dogs*. But that was just humour, to me, from Burroughs, a guy who was a crazy, brilliant heroin addict.

But David picked different people at different times and he absorbed all he could out of them energetically, and then he would go on to the next, the next, the next. He was a chameleon, he was an artist, he was a searcher – almost like a researcher of music and multimedia; it wasn't just like being in a rock band.

David's guitar-playing on *Diamond Dogs* is underrated. Is it Jeff Beck? No. Is it John McLaughlin? No, but it didn't have to be. It was raw and honest, and then you put my classy piano-playing on top of it – it's pure genius. That's what I'm talking about; that's the fusion that I was alluding to. That's where he had no fear.

We were like minds, even though our lifestyles were very different, especially at the beginning. You've got to understand I was not into any drugs, so I'm totally almost an enemy to that world.

Remember, I didn't care for rock rock 'n' roll. I didn't know who David Bowie was. I'm a serious jazz and classical musician and composer – a very good pianist – and this just wasn't my world at that time.

Jazz audiences are very polite. Fans at a jazz club will come up and shake your hand. But rock fans – man, that's a whole other thing. I never really figured it out when people use the phrase "You're a rock star". To this day, I've never thought of myself that way; I can hardly get my thoughts around that when somebody says it.

But I played with a rock icon and I'm part of that music: I was the longest member in the band when you put all the hours and tours together; played on the most albums and did the most concerts. So we're talking 19 albums, we're talking about probably 400 or 500 concerts; we're talking about probably 200 to 300 days of rehearsals in studios. I did his first American show and his last one with Alicia Keys in 2006 in America. And I had only been hired for eight weeks!

I always thought there would be another tour – there were incomplete projects that he talked to me about doing that we never did.

——

I never could tell this to anybody since 1996. I was not able to say this because it would have been crazy and alarming, but David told it to me on the bus late at night when nobody was listening. He said he had seen a psychic five or six or seven years earlier who told him he was going to die at around age 69.

He told it to me, he didn't question it at all; he knew it. So consequently he plants that in my head and I'm waiting for it. So now we're at that time, in January of 2016. I get the call and go into shock, which is a normal human reaction, and ten seconds later I said, "Oh, that's what he told me." This is separate from him knowing for 18 months he was dying of liver cancer, mind you: that I didn't know, he didn't tell me that.

Just imagine, that he had this information for many years, and he planned his whole life accordingly.

Look, we all die, but not everybody knows when. So you can extend that awareness of his mortality he showed on *Blackstar* back many, many years. Prior to that he told me in 2004, "Mike, we won't be touring for the next ten years because I want to be there as my daughter, Lexi, grows up; I want to be there for her. I wasn't there for Duncan that way; I want to do it for her." And he did.

Everyone's asking me for ten years, "Why are you not touring?" Well, the truth of the matter is I always knew exactly why: it was because he wanted to be with his daughter. And that was a very sane decision, especially if he knows he's going to die. I mention it again because that's part of David Bowie's mystique. I might be the only person he told that to. I don't know if he ever shared that with Iman. Some day I'll ask her.

———

David was involved in the pop market and he knew about being commercial, and he told me the smartest thing that anyone ever said to me, and I'm finally applying it at 70 years old. We were at SIR studios in Manhattan in '95, and we're sitting around, and he said, "Mike, you know what separates you from me and Mick Jagger?" I'm thinking, What? Well, you're both skinnier than me, you both can sing, you're both rock stars, I'm a piano player. He said, "What separates me and Mick from you is we're great businessmen and you're not." So honest that I couldn't even get it.

I didn't believe him. But I didn't believe my dad when he was alive, who said my problem is I don't do any PR for myself. When I look back now, as I finally grab a few pieces of wisdom at 70, I realize that somehow for the last 60 years I've just been supporting other artists – David being the main one, David being the best of all.

———

MOONAGE DAYDREAM – MICK ROCK (1972)

Artwork based on one of Mick's own photos of Bowie taken in 1973 © Mick Rock, 1994, 2016.
Mick Rock had unprecedented access to Bowie during the Ziggy era, shooting him throughout
his tours in the UK and the US. The collage depicts David with the "Third Eye" exaggeration he
picked up from Calvin Mark Lee, an A&R man with Mercury Records.

I'm starting now to actually do my own thing and it's quite interesting because you don't expect that, you expect a guy at 70 to retire, and I'm more vitalized than when I was 20.

It's a crazy thing: David originally hired me for eight weeks. He fired five bands in that first two years: most of those musicians were excellent, but they were good at one thing. Because I was a fusion musician, I could do "Young Americans" and play gospel and yet also do the simplest piano-playing and come up with a Latin thing on "Young Americans"; I also could play "Aladdin Sane". So I could play groove music, rhythm and blues, pop, gospel and, like him, I made them all my own.

So the bottom line was, David did fire these other guys, but he couldn't fire me. I made it all the way to the *Young Americans* tour, when I was the musical director with Luther Vandross and Dave Sanborn and all that. We called that group the Mike Garson Band, and we were our own opening act, with Robin Clark and Luther Vandross fronting us instead of David – we played a half hour and we got booed off half the time. It was only after that tour, when he did *The Man who Fell to Earth,* that I went back to playing jazz.

It was kind of predestined that in 1992, for *Black Tie White Noise* and *Buddha of Suburbia*, he called me again and we got back together because we hadn't finished what we had to do. He was so good at pulling the best out of everybody as a producer and a casting director, that every style of music I could play, he utilized.

———

Ultimately, the best answer to what made David Bowie different from other musicians is, I think, he had a wider window. He had a wider perception.

History will see David as a musician, a producer, a singer, a performer, a writer, an actor, an artist, a painter, a sculptor, an editor of an art magazine, a Renaissance man, a philosopher – you know, somewhat a pessimist at times and somewhat an optimist at times. The fact that his stroke was so wide helps separates him from his peers, from other great singers, for example. He just wasn't like any of these other people: I never saw him as a rock musician.

Toni Basil

When she met David Bowie, Toni Basil was best known as a dancer, choreographer and member of legendary street dance group The Lockers. She choreographed his Diamond Dogs *tour (1974) and* Glass Spider *tour (1987). Toni Basil went on to become a singer–songwriter, actress and film director. She sang the multi-million selling hit "Mickey".*

I started working with David at a turning point for him, in 1974, when he went from Ziggy to the tight pants and the suit. I remember opening night: half his fans were dressed as Ziggy and, oh my God, did they get a surprise.

Around that time I had been choreographing for television and I also had put together a group of dancers with Don Campbell from South L.A., called The Lockers – it was based on a dance that he created called the Campbell Lock. We had been working on it for a couple of years, but it all came together in '73 and they were absolutely huge on TV. We broke down all the barriers, and convinced the mainstream that street dance was a true American art form.

We showed everyone what was coming out of the urban American community, and the kids there learned that they could earn a living with their art. It took us a couple of years but getting on TV was our big break. We toured with Frank Sinatra, and opened for him at Carnegie Hall the same year we opened up for Funkadelic at Radio City Music Hall.

PIN UPS – JUSTIN DE VILLENEUVE (1973)

This image of Twiggy and David was originally planned for Vogue. *David had wanted to be the first man on the cover of* Vogue *and Justin de Villeneuve arranged a shoot in Paris where Bowie was working on the album* Pin Ups. *The "masks" were suggested by Justin's make up lady as a way of dealing with the contrasting skin colours (Twiggy had a tan having recently been on holiday). On seeing the Polaroids, David asked if he could use them for the album cover and the photographer agreed.* Vogue *never spoke to Justin again.*

Angie Bowie saw the group, and she told David about us – he had the same agent as I did, too. Next thing, I was flown to London to meet him. I thought he was drop-dead gorgeous! I felt like I was there to meet him and discuss a possible future project, but I wasn't sure what it was. He never mentioned a project. The idea was just to get to know me and my ideas, and he sent me to see the original *Rocky Horror Show* when it was at the King's Road Theatre, and it was considered the hippest thing. He said, "You've got to see that."

I certainly knew about him and his music before I met him. I was deep into R&B by then because I was street dancing, but I was very enamoured with his theatricality. He was the first one who brought performance art into rock 'n' roll, really way ahead of his time. And before I went to London I asked the agency, "What can I see of his that I haven't seen?" And they showed me a screening of the D.A. Pennebaker concert documentary *Ziggy Stardust and the Spiders from Mars*.

I think halfway through it I screamed out, "Oh my God, he's straight!" Because everybody was questioning: was he androgynous? What was he? And knowing he was straight made him so, so much more interesting, because he had absolutely no fear of experimenting with his image. He didn't care if people thought he was gay or straight – he was just about his art.

We got along great, to say the least. I came back to LA and then I got a call from my agent saying, "Hey, David wants you to come to New York to choreograph his opening number for the *Diamond Dogs* tour." So I said, "I'm going to be there for a long time because I'm going to do the whole show." I just knew that. I knew it, I knew that he and I were in alignment on what our aesthetics were. I was not just a ballet dancer, but a street dancer as well. I covered a real wide range of territory. I was brought up in the theatre so I knew all old-school stuff, and I also studied living theatre and open theatre.

David walked the line of mime, you know, because he had studied mime with Lindsay Kemp, and he was a glutton for doing homework. He just loved to know everything that was going on and then stay one step ahead. So I just knew it was going to happen for the two of us. And it did. It absolutely did.

I knew this tour was going to be something so special and I wanted so much to be working with him, because I had never really worked on such a big pop production. And I think it was one of the first pop-music productions of its kind.

When I met him in New York, I was standing in a pair of peg pants and he said to me, "Where did you get those pants?" And I said, "At Jenny Waterbags", and we went to Jenny Waterbags. A friend of mine owned the shop, and he got himself an outfit for the opening.

———

When I showed up that day in that hotel in New York, I had a plan. I was armed with ideas. It was just so much fun for me, because I knew we could make it great and what he was looking for I could fill in, and what he gave me I could run with.

By the time I saw him in New York, he had a whole set; the structure and the ideas and the bridge and the cherry picker coming down when he sang "Space Oddity" – that was all there when I arrived. He didn't explain it, he just showed me the set; I showed him pictures and we just took it song by song. Some songs, like "Space Oddity", with the cherry picker, were already structured in ideas, and other things would just come out of our heads.

I went there with some ideas of big shadows over buildings. I showed him drawings and tracings of Magritte and Man Ray. At the opening of that show, his big silhouette comes on. We talked about lighting and they said, "We can do it with the barn door" – really old school, the barn door down, the lights down at the edge of the stage. As he goes closer and further away from the light it gets bigger and smaller, and it was really quite effective at the time.

I had to stay up nights putting it all together. I had to do so much homework. Trying

to figure out the time signature of the opening of "Big Brother" was totally impossible. I had to go to Michael Kamen – Bowie's musical director – in the morning and say, "OK, I give up, I can't count the opening of 'Big Brother'!"

I just took each song as it came; I dealt with it visually. I think the reason I was brought in was because he was also talking to Michael Bennett, who choreographed *A Chorus Line*, etc., at the time, and I think David had talked to him about the "Diamond Dogs" song.

David wanted to have two guys on leashes, and I think Michael was uncomfortable with it. I can't really speak for Michael, but I know when David had started to talk to me that same day that I met him in the hotel room in New York he said, "Well, can we do 'Diamond Dogs' with the guys on leashes?" and I said, "Absolutely, why not?!" And he screamed to Corinne Schwab – his long-time assistant: "Corinne! The dogs are back in! The dogs are back in the show!"

But my concept was incredibly long ropes. The idea was that David would be standing on the bridge, which was maybe two storeys up, and throw the leashes down, and the dogs will run around and make geometric shapes.

And then once the bridge lowered David to the stage, the dogs end up wrapping him in the ropes – which was a total reversal of what people might expect. I mean, that's what theatre's about: the element of surprise.

After "Diamond Dogs" the next song up was "Panic in Detroit". One day we were in rehearsal, finishing "Diamond Dogs," and David was wrapped in these ropes, on his knees, and then all of a sudden it was like I saw a cartoon lightbulb turn on over his head.

ZIGGY '73 – RICHARD IMRIE (1973)

Ziggy as photographed in January, 1973 by Richard Imrie. Bowie had returned to the UK for a short tour and to put the finishing touches to the album Aladdin Sane, *which was finished on the 24th January and released in the UK in April that year.*

The look on his face was like, "Oh my God, I have an idea." And he got up, he unwrapped himself, he grabbed the chairs that were in the room – there were just a few chairs, we were in a rehearsal room – and he made himself a boxing ring out of those ropes. He had been boxing with his trainer. And once again, that's how his brain worked – the whole time he was training, he was wondering, where would this go, could he use it for something? So he sang "Panic in Detroit" with boxing gloves on, in a boxing ring that he made out of the "Diamond Dogs" ropes. I screamed to him: "Knock yourself out at the end, before you finish the song." And he knocked himself out at the end – he created that, and then I gave him an ending, in the 3 minutes and 40 seconds that the song took. I think it's because we both came from the same kind of theatre; we both understood improvisational and spontaneous ideas. We were able to make things up instantaneously.

He was such a great actor. His shows were not about listening to the rock 'n' roll singer standing there; there was so much more going on. Oh my God, he just covered all the bases. He was just the prettiest boy, he was prettier than any woman or man in the room, always. Where do you go from there?

I went to the Philadelphia opening for *Diamond Dogs*, and I was on for a couple of other of the shows. When we were finished he gave me a present, and the present was that he was giving me co-director's credit. That was incredible, really generous, and kind of proof that there was quite a collaboration that went on.

———

It was 14 years before I worked with him again on *Glass Spider*, but I heard from him in the meantime – he'd reach out from time to time. I had "Mickey" in between, the one enormous hit that doesn't go away. He did get in touch with me for the Nile Rodgers-produced album *Let's Dance*, but I was in the middle of my short musical-video career.

DAVID LIVE (1974)

Bowie is bound during the Diamond Dogs tour in 1974. The show toured Canada and the US for nearly six months with a month's break in August for David to work on Young Americans. *The show was one of the most visually spectacular the world had seen, thanks in part to the complexity of the set – an interpretation of Hunger City in the style of German artist George Grosz. The July shows in Philadelphia were recorded to create David's first live album –* David Live.

I became a pop star because I had worked for Bowie. I was in the middle of working with the Lockers, and I just thought, I want to sing; I had a bigger idea for dance in pop and so I started putting on these shows, and the first show was songs I'd choreographed for other people that I'd always wanted to do myself. So I got a record deal from an English company.

Tina Turner had asked me to do something, too, and I had to turn her down. I'd worked for Tina for years before, and of course I've worked for her since, but I think David and Tina were glad when I didn't have a big second hit: I could come back and work for them! Which I did.

It was stressful to be in the middle of what Tina and David did, which was create their shows and then have to go out and do them. I was really more of a video performer.

But with David and Tina, you had people who could sing and move – who created the whole thing. And trust me, David Bowie, he almost didn't need any others – he didn't need the set designer, he didn't need the lighting guy, he didn't need me, because he could do all of these jobs himself. I'd seen him solve other people's problems. But it's too much. You really need to have a collaborator on every avenue, otherwise there's no way you can do it.

The creation of *Diamond Dogs* was a similar experience to *Glass Spider* in many ways – even touching on some of the same ideas – because he always was what he was, from the very beginning. Maybe on *Diamond Dogs* I hadn't applied my talents in that exact way before, and maybe I looked behind my back a little bit more, was more wary of what could go wrong. *Glass Spider* was a bigger set, obviously; you have that glass spider come

---

SCISSORS – TERRY O'NEILL (1974)

*This shot was taken at Terry O'Neill's first photoshoot with Bowie, to promote the album
Diamond Dogs in 1974. O'Neill would go on to photograph him throughout the tour.
The photographer was delighted when the singer turned up in a mustard suit. When David
absent-mindedly picked up a pair of scissors, he carried on shooting, feeling they symbolised
his "cutting edge music".*

down. It was quite, quite physical. David used street dancers so it was different – the tour after he used LaLaLa Human Steps, who were fantastic: he was always one step ahead. He always knew what was going on, even before YouTube!

You didn't give David Bowie choreography: you gave him back what you knew he could do. He was a mime; you knew how he moved. You give Tina Turner back her steps and you kind of know how far out she can go outside her own comfort zone. But you didn't expect them to do what I can do, because I sure as hell couldn't do what they could do. David was improvisational also, so you gave him ideas and steps in many songs, he could use them if he wanted, and yet he didn't have to. You wanted to keep him free.

I knew he did party hard, but I didn't get to be included in the partying – I've never been that person. It never interfered with our daily work, though – there was never a day where rehearsal was cancelled, ever. I don't ever remember anything like that. The work ethic was always there.

After *Glass Spider* we stayed in touch on email. Every now and then, twice a year maybe, if he saw something interesting, or if he thought somebody stole something from us, he would email me. We emailed about one of the dancers who he really adored, Skeeter Rabbit, a brilliant, brilliant street dancer who was on the *Glass Spider* tour – very, very authentic, drop-dead gorgeous and manic depressive. Quite genius; quite, quite extraordinary. David really took to him, just adored him, and when Skeet killed himself, David and I were both heartbroken.

I emailed him during the London Olympics, when he opened and closed the show, although he wasn't even there, you know, it was all on the screen. I just said: you're the only one that could open the show, close the show and not show up!

David emailed me last September, it was around my birthday, and he just said, "How you doing, darling; what are you doing?" Sometimes he would send emails and you would send an email back that he wouldn't answer. That happened a lot. He would just disappear; he was notorious for that. When he emailed, of course, the email address was not David Bowie, and if you didn't get one for a year and you get a million emails a day like I do, you would look at the email address before you delete it and go, "God, this looks familiar to me," and then go "Ohh, gosh, it's David Bowie!" And I would become beside myself with excitement that he had emailed me! Because you're just always a fan. I was always a fan.

He did disappear after he worked with you because he'd moved on to the next thing. The same thing happens when you work on movies: you become really friendly with an actor, and you say, "We'll have dinner and we'll have lunch" and then it never happens. So when David did reach out in emails, you'd get all puffed up, and think, "Wow, I'm the best thing in the world".

My work with David was one of the most important creative collaborations that I had ever experienced. What we accomplished, what I got to accomplish with him, what he allowed me to do – it was just incredible. He let me in and gave me that co-director's credit – and ended up doing the same thing on on Glass Spider, which was fantastic. It was a surprise in the playbill; it was like it was my gift. I mean, holy God.

Earl Slick

US blues and rock guitar virtuoso Earl Slick has played with David Bowie, John Lennon, the New York Dolls and Yoko Ono, among others. While he was initially brought onboard by David Bowie to replace Mick Ronson for the Diamond Dogs *tour, it was to become a fruitful and enduring relationship, with Slick continuing to work with Bowie through to* The Next Day *(2013).*

Meeting David, it was like I'd walked on to a *Twilight Zone* set. Before that, I'd really been doing blues and rock n' roll – I was a very serious-assed blues guy. David was a whole other world.

I had a friend named Michael Kamen, God rest his soul, who became a very, very famous movie composer. Michael was my mentor. A friend introduced me to him and Michael took me under his wing and showed me the ropes. He was a Juilliard graduate and he was already writing pieces of music, classical shit – he'd written some music for the Joffrey Ballet. David had gone to see it, he met Michael backstage, and David says to Michael, "My guitar player, Mick Ronson, just left the band, I need a guy, you got anybody?" And Mike said, "Yes, I do", and he called me. And then Michael said, "I got something for you, so get your shit together."

Then I got a call from Bowie's assistant, Corinne Schwab, setting up an audition at RCA, and so I walked in and they asked me what amp I wanted and all that. They were actually in the process of playing back and I think doing some finishing touches on mixing the *Diamond Dogs* album – not the live one, obviously, because that was done

---

HERO – MASAYOSHI SUKITA (1977)

Starting in 1972 Masayoshi Sukita had a 40-year association with Bowie and produced many of the famous images of the artist. This photo comes from a photoshoot in 1977. Bowie had come to Japan to promote Iggy Pop's album The Idiot. *He had a one-hour photo session with Masayoshi and wanted the shots to have a punk feel – he'd asked fashion stylist Yacco Takahashi to order in plenty of leather jackets. From this shoot came the iconic cover shot of* "Heroes".

with me. They brought me right into the studio. There was a Marshall in there and some headphones: I put the headphones on, I hear a voice come over the headphones, and I can't see, the control room's black. They blacked it out; I couldn't see who the fuck I was talking to, right? It was an American accent, so it possibly was the producer, Tony Visconti. And he said, "Hi". David didn't say anything; I didn't hear his voice at all.

They told me to play along to a couple of tracks. I asked what key they were in, they said, oh don't worry about that, just play along. So I just played along with some tracks: one of them was "Diamond Dogs", and maybe one or two other bits they had from that album, about 10, maybe 15, minutes. There was very little dialogue. And then David came in the room and sat down, and I remember grabbing a bottle of brandy out of my breast pocket and storing it down on the amp, and he picked up his guitar, and we sort of sat around and bullshitted and played guitars for maybe a half hour. And he thanked me for coming and Corinne Schwab said, "We'll give you a call in a couple of weeks, we've got about a dozen guys to look at", and I went "Oh, fuck, man, that's going to be a long two weeks." Anyway, luckily, the next morning the phone rang: "Yeah, David liked what you did yesterday so if you'd like to do this, he'd like you, so why don't you come into town and meet?" Which I did.

Really, all I knew about him ahead of that was that I really loved the *Aladdin Sane* record. I wasn't, per se, a Bowie fan. I was quite aware of him and there were a couple of things, like *Ziggy*, that I liked. Actually, I owned *Hunky Dory* and *Aladdin Sane* at the time, it's all I had. Obviously I knew he was a major fucking star, but I could see that he was not done – you could see that he was already big but he was going to go beyond that.

I'd no preconceived ideas about who he was, what he was, or any other thing. So there were no expectations of any kind. He was very nice and cordial and cool, and that was it.

I definitely learned a lot about how to be a professional and how to function in the music industry from him over the years; I'd learn new shit all the time. But, initially,

THE DUKE AND THE EARL (1974)

Earl Slick worked with Bowie on and off for nearly 40 years. Brought in for the Diamond Dogs tour in 1974, he played on Young Americans *(1975),* Station to Station *(1976),* Heathen *(2002),* Reality *(2003) and* The Next Day *(2013) as well as playing guitar during the Serious Moonlight tour in 1983.*

when I came in, my biggest fright was that he was going to have me cop all of Ronson's stuff, and I thought, Well, you know, I love Mick's playing and we have similarities but you could tell Mick and me a mile apart, easy. And when I asked him about that as we were getting ready to go on tour, he said, I want you to do your take on these, so just learn the songs, take them on and do what you would do. That was it: that was all my instruction.

So I went OK, that's cool, and I watched him. I watched him make some really bad mistakes; I watched him do some very brilliant things. And, you know, every once in a while he would throw out some kind of words of wisdom at me. One of them, which I stand by to this day, is to say what you mean, mean what you say, say it once and shut the fuck up. And that goes across the board: business, press, band, you name it. And that's a rule I've never broken – I've done the least amount of press since his demise.

———

In those early days, I think that in the midst of the hunger for stardom and getting hooked up with a guy like Tony Defries, who had more money than God, David was walking around and living like he'd already sold 80 million records when he was 25 years old. Funded by MainMan, which was Tony Defries. I don't think David had a grip on the reality of that and I think because of that a lot of shit got past him. Not to mention, and this is common knowledge, the fucking drugs didn't help either.

We were all at it. You get a kid who's 25 years old, especially somebody like him who knew very well how to manipulate audiences – he was a great performer, on and off the stage – and I think he started believing his own shit after a while. In the course of that I think he just let stuff go, and people took advantage of him.

Doing the *Diamond Dogs* tour I was in over my head: I'm on stage with David Bowie, with Michael Kamen and David Sanborn, who I knew because we'd all played in a band together earlier. I did not know Mike Garson, but I knew of him and, man, his work was amazing. I was very familiar with Herbie Flowers and Tony Newman from Herbie's work with David and both of them with T. Rex. I was on the stage with guys who were a lot older than me, and a lot more experienced than me, who all had names, and I was the new kid: I was hungry to learn from these guys. And doing those shows was fucking great. I was like a kid in a candy store: doing big shows, doing what fucking 22-year-old kids do when they're in a spot like that, having a fucking blast. OK, I'd been on a couple of records before on some major labels, sitting in as a sideman, but I'd never done anything like this. I mean, the first guy I get with, I end up with a gold record?

When we did *Station to Station*, at the time I couldn't make heads or tails what he was doing. I was going: "What the fuck are we doing? I kind of liked what we were doing before." I don't know if David sometimes would just get bored with it... He liked to push himself into a new direction, for the sake of putting himself in the middle of a fire; in other words, pushing himself to the limits to create something new. He did that until the day he died. David was not going to be satisfied unless the new work was new work, not a different version of the last album.

I'm very similar to him in the way that what happened before is really not important: I don't sit here and talk about the past all day, I'm talking about what I'm doing next. And David was very much like that. What am I doing now? What's the new thing? What's going to float my boat this time, you know?

And there wasn't a whole lot of discussion about it on *Station to Station*. It just kind of happened. All of a sudden, oh, this is what we're doing. No matter how you cut the cake, as important as the band is to each record and to each tour David did, it's still him: he's the boss. If you work for Microsoft you don't go to Bill Gates and tell him what to do. Bill Gates tells you what to do and you figure it out. I had enough street smarts in me to understand that; a lot of guys didn't. And I was like, OK, well, we're changing directions here, it is what it is. Go forth.

DAVID AND EARL (2000)

The artist and the guitarist together at the BBC Radio Theatre in 2000. They would follow up this show with the headline slot at the Glastonbury Festival – a performance described by founder Michael Eavis as "one of the best appearances in the history of the event." It was a major change from his first appearance at the inaugural festival in 1971 when, due to delays and concerns over neighbours complaining about the noise, Bowie's 9pm show didn't kick off until dawn.

It was actually a lot easier working with him then than it was on *Young Americans* because the music we were doing was a lot easier for me to get into. And also it was a small band. There was just two guitars, a bass and drums, and I brought [keyboardist] Roy Bittan in to play. I don't think Roy could have been there more than maybe two days, so the rest of the time we did the basic tracks, and a lot of the time it was just me and David in the studio doing overdubs. And we were both equally out there, but somehow – don't ask me, I don't know how the fuck we made that record. We had youth going for us: your body could take a hammering; seriously could take a fucking hammering. He and I were the two out of the band that were out of control all of the time. I was just as out of control as he was. But it probably helped. I didn't realize how weird he was until years later when I was like, wow, he was really freewheeling during that period. Bowie went: "So were you, dude".

That said, he was not as out of control as he was made out to be, in terms of his functionality. When he got his mind into something he could hyper-focus like a motherfucker. I don't care if he was living on milk and I don't know fucking what, it didn't matter. When he got a mind on, it got done, always. He always had the ability to do that. And so did I at the time. On that record we didn't discuss anything, there was no plan; we went in and we just started cutting tracks. It's not like now when people sit around and talk and fucking send MP3s back and forth all day. Just get the band in the studio and fucking make a record –that's the way to do it. And that's all we did. The record took on a life of its own as it went on.

━━━━━

There was a long break after *Station to Station* – there were some cunts on the business side pulling some fast ones, and playing David and me against each other. And there was a major, major snafu on both my and David's parts, not knowing what was going on – in come the drugs again – not knowing that we were both being manipulated and fucked with. We were both getting different stories from different people, and I bailed. I couldn't even get him on the phone, nobody would let me talk to him, and I thought, You know what, this is bullshit.

It was us getting taken advantage of and manipulated by people, and pitted against each other. I know what the reasons were, which right now are irrelevant, but that's pretty much what happened: it was a big-ass misunderstanding. Had either one of us known what the fuck was going on I never would have left. That was a mistake on my part, a whopper of a mistake.

Around seven years later, Stevie Ray Vaughan backs out of a tour with David, and I was always the go-to guy when the shit hit the fan. I got a call asking if I could get to Brussels in the next 48 hours. They got together the work papers and whatever, and I flew over. There were maybe just dress rehearsals before the first show, and I remember that's when DB and I cleared up the mess from 1976, because we had to clear the air; I mean, there was no way we could have worked together without that coming up. So we went out, we talked about it and cleared all that up. He says, "Can you have this together by the US Festival?", which was like two or three weeks in to the tour… I said, "No, I'll have it together on the first show." So I basically stayed in my room and I pretty much got an insane two-hour show together in two days. There had been that seven-year gap and a lot of that stuff I'd never played on before, so I had to learn the shit.

By this point in time, David's feet were way more on the ground: he was keeping his shit together, and I was as well, even though – trust me – we were not angels. But there's no way that we could have gone on such a long tour and pulled it off the way we did if we were anything close to the condition we were in when making *Station to Station*. There's just no fucking way. It was toned down to a point that was manageable.

So we did the tour in '83, then he went to do the *Tonight* record, which I was supposed to do. But I didn't hear anything, and I'm going, what the fuck? Turned out they were making the record and they just didn't bother to call me. He would do shit like that: no grudge, it was just the way he was. You took David the way he was or you took a hike.

I chose to take the experiences as they came and take them seriously, because I loved working with him, and I loved him as a guy. Things that might have turned others into resentful, hateful people against him just didn't with me. That's not to say that it didn't piss me off once or twice, it did – but not to the point where I wouldn't work with him again. He was never vindictive, he just did what he did; he was just him. He worked with who suited him at the time. One thing he was very good about was that once he knew in his head what kind of record he was going to make, or roughly what kind of record, he would call guys that could do that. In other words, if he is going to make an electronic record, or shit like that, he's not going to call me, he's going to call [Robert] Fripp, [Adrian] Belew, David Torn. That's not my shit, he knows that's not my shit. It's his career, it's his deal. He can pick and choose who he wants when he wants, and he's got a complete right to do that and you've really got nothing to bitch about.

At the very end of '99, the webmaster of my site called me to say he'd just got an email from this person and he said he didn't know who it was. It was a 212 number and the company was Isolar. I knew right away what it was. I called them – this was right around when Reeves Gabrels had left, and David had gone through a few guitar players. Then in the beginning of 2000, I flew to New York and met with him and the band and we played together, and we started working again. When I walked into the room it was like I'd seen him yesterday. You just pick right up.

———

Those years were a blast. I've got to say that everything we did after the turn of the century was great, because we were both cleaned up, 100 per cent, on our game. Things were good and it was fun. He was still him, but he was a lot more hands-on with stuff. For instance, on the *Reality* record – he made that record in pieces, it wasn't like the whole band got together on that – one day I'm just working at home on my solo album, *Zig Zag*, and he said, "What are you doing?" I said, "I'm hanging out with the dogs."

"Well, get in the car and come on down, I need some shit done." So I jumped in the car, went down, we worked for a couple of days – that's something that would never happen before; it used to be that a manager or someone else would call or email me. In the past there was always a go-between. Having that direct contact made it a little simpler.

The thing about my relationship with him is that I kept up a certain distance. And that was a calculated distance. We were friends, we were good friends, we understood each other very well, inside and out, but I wasn't the guy that was going to email him and go "Let's go to a show, let's hang out." I never did that. I never wanted to do that. I thought, You know what, we've got a good relationship the way this is working. And when we work, we're friends, we're all buddies; it's all fucking cool. In between, I would rather just live my own life, and, you know, I don't really want to be part of his life in between work. That might sound a little crude to people if they read that, but it was only for the reason that I had seen what had happened with a few of the moths who got too close to the flame. He would go sideways, in a different way than when it went sideways between him and me.

I didn't want to be the go-to guy as far as his day-to-day shit went. I didn't want to be that right-hand guy who had to be there all the time on call. My biggest goal in life was not to be his best friend. I just left him alone, and he left me alone, and I think we had an unspoken agreement where we both thought pretty much the same way, and I felt a lot better about things that way. That way, if things go sideways then you don't take it personally. Because things go sideways on occasion in any relationship of any kind that you're in. With someone like David, where it's not just his living at stake, it's his emotional wellbeing, it's the perception that the outside has looking in. So I was always my own man, as he was his, and I think that unspoken agreement served us well.

I remember, working on the track "Valentine's Day" for *The Next Day*, he would use my hands with his brain; in other words, his head was hearing it but he couldn't do it on the guitar. So he would give me a rough – he would play it to me roughly or hum it to me – and then I would figure out what to do with it. So it was very much a back-and-forth, give-and-take thing, where sometimes it was my ideas, sometimes it was his ideas, and it wasn't a matter of ego, of whose parts were used, it was what worked, what made the song better.

The first thing I said – when I heard how the chord change works as part of the melody – was, "This is the fucking Kinks, man". And his eyes lit up, he says, "Fuck, yeah". If you listen to my rhythm guitar on there you're going to hear little "Waterloo Sunset" bits underneath there. And pretty much all the stuff we did together, when we talked of references, we were both on the same page. Because we did like a lot of the same things. We both loved the Kinks, and he was a Keith Richards fan, just like me.

You know, I mean, if you listen to the solo in "Station to Station", where we go up tempo, the whole front end of that solo is Chuck Berry. And even though I'm using this gnarly, fuzzy sound on the "Reality" title track, you can hear Keith all over that fucking thing, because that's what he saw in that one, too. So there'd be references of things we both liked and were familiar with.

The *Reality* tour ended unexpectedly – the weirdest thing was that he was perfectly fine and then all of a sudden he was perfectly not fine, out of nowhere. So then the heart attack happened, I figured, OK, it'll take him a while to figure out what he wants to do. And there were about three or four close calls where I did get phone calls and I was put on hold to tour, but it didn't happen.

I think that not long after he had the heart attack, he honestly was just going to recuperate and go about his business, but as the aftermath of that became a reality something changed. I would never ask him or pry; that was not my business. As time went on, maybe he was interested in doing some other shit, or didn't want to go out. I mean, I can't guess, because there were parts of David that you never could get through. Same with me, a lot of people can't read me: we were similar that way.

———

The last time I saw him was the last day that we worked on *The Next Day* album, which would have been 25 July, 2012, I think. I did my last overdubs and he had some of the staff coming getting the stuff out of the studio, and that was that. Afterwards we exchanged the occasional email every now and then.

I got an email from him, and a phone call, a few months before he died. I guess it was his goodbye, but in his own way, and I had no idea that's what was happening until 10 January, then I figured out what had happened. It was my birthday when he called: he didn't always remember. He just did a quick happy-birthday email and I just responded with a smiley face and the phone rang a few hours later: "Oh, I just thought I'd give you a quick holler anyway ... Happy birthday, have a great time, whatever, and I'll see you when I see you." That was that. "OK, boss, later. Bye." I mean, it was that quick of a phone call. But that had never happened before: I never got a phone call and an email on my birthday. So I guess that's what that was.

Thinking about what made Bowie Bowie, first of all, obviously, the talent was there, so that goes without saying. He was very driven and very focused when he was doing things, and he had this magic to him. There was something there that other people just don't have. I can't even tell you what that is; I used to call it the little pixie dust. Some people have this magic, and he had it. And I think the length of his career is largely due to the fact that he was driven to change all the time. And part of it is being a solo artist.

Take the Rolling Stones, right? They're my favourite band on the fucking planet. What has made them is that they do what I love to do, which is be on a motherfucking stage. That's why the Rolling Stones are the Rolling Stones, dedicated to what they do and they do one thing, and they do it like no other motherfucker on the planet can

---

THE LODGER'S DRESSING ROOM – BRIAN DUFFY (1979)

David in the dressing room at the shoot for the cover of Lodger *in 1979. The album cover was art directed by Derek Boshier and shot by Brian Duffy.* Lodger *was the last of the "Berlin Trilogy" (a possibly loose term given* "Heroes" *is the only one of the three fully recorded at the Hansa Studio by the Wall, Berlin –* Low *was mostly recorded in France,* Lodger *in Switzerland and New York).*

do it. It's the same thing David did but only in his own way, because there was no definitive band that he stuck with: he was a solo artist, so he could not get away with what the Stones did.

I mean, think about it. If you go back to the beginning of the Stones and you go all the way to today, and you look at their fucking set list, right? There's a lot of shit in there that they've played a thousand times, ten thousand times. And it's with the same ferocity, it's a ferocious fucking band, but it's a band. Whereas David being a solo artist, to keep things going like that, you've got to make changes. Look at Sinatra, for instance, his crooning period at the beginning – he was the first rock star, in my mind – and then he diversified a little bit, he went to movies, and that worked really well for him.

Sinatra's look changed over the years, too: he did the Rat Pack thing, which is a whole other departure from being the teenage idol he was in the Forties, and David almost followed that, if you think about it, but way more drastically. I mean, listen to *Low* and listen to *Ziggy* – they sound like they come out of two completely different people.

And he did, in his time, write some iconic songs that people are never going to forget. It really boils down to that with the Stones, too – they're the best live band ever in history, but the songs are still there. It's the songs that made them what they are. You listen to "Satisfaction", or "Ruby Tuesday", and who the fuck is going to forget that? And David had that: so many identifiably great songs that aren't all in the same vein, "Ziggy", "Life on Mars", "Rebel Rebel", "Jean Genie", "Young Americans", "Fame". I mean, Christ!

———

So many times I'm asked to describe him in a sentence or a word and I never can. I can't. He was too much of a multi-faceted motherfucker. To say he was this, that or the other thing is just impossible: he was a lot of things all at once. I've seen his paintings, I've seen his poetry, I've heard the music, I've seen the acting... He was interested in a lot of things, some of them he did better than others. Nobody does everything great, but one thing that I've seen him do, that I've seen very few people on this planet can do, is to get on the stage and control a fucking audience like he did. It was fucking ridiculous. I've never seen anybody be able to relate to and take an audience through 20 different fucking frames of mind and emotional states in one show: *that* he could do.

As time went on, and on the later tours, he was even more personable with the audience. He was more of the same guy that he was with us on the bus. We had a couple of buses, and we'd sit in the back and he'd tell some dumb-ass stupid jokes, right, and I would tell dumb-ass stupid jokes, and then he would actually start using my jokes onstage, talking to the audience. I'm going, what the fuck, man? He should pay me for that shit! And we'd laugh. But if you look at some of the footage of those later tours, he would goof around a bit more, and that would be the David that you would be hanging out with in the back of the bus. That was the biggest change that I saw from the old days: he was much more willing to be more vulnerable, laugh, be laughed at, be laughed with, whatever you want to call it.

There were times when I avoided him like the fucking plague, in the Seventies, but that was all just drug moods. And, trust me, I had mine. It was the drugs we were doing, because I would be the same way a lot of times. People would fucking steer damn clear of me! And you know what, it may be hard to imagine that he was humble, but he was. He always was but it was more evident as he got older, because it wasn't being masked by manipulative people and drugs.

I would say over the whole period of 40-something years, maybe two or three times we had some pretty personal moments that we shared; very few. It was usually when one of us might be down in the dumps or something would happen and it would get discussed. I remember when we hadn't seen each other for God knows how long, when I came back in the band in 2000, in those first few gigs, you could see it: we'd look at

each other and that big smile would come on our faces, you know, it would be like, Yeah! At one point, David said, "nobody else plays 'Fame' like Slicky", and that to me was worth its weight in gold.

Some things I've said might seem a little off colour, but that's because even though David's passed away he was a real guy, and real people aren't OK all the time. They aren't nice all the time. He was an anomaly, without a doubt. I never met anybody like him in my life, whether be it personally or professionally. He was a one-of-a-kind deal.

PIERROT – BRIAN DUFFY (1980)

Designed by lifelong friend Natasha Korniloff, the Pierrot costume was worn by David on the cover of Scary Monsters (and Super Creeps) *and in the famous "Ashes to Ashes" video. The Pierrot character had featured before in David's past. He made his stage debut as Cloud in mime artist Lindsey Kemp's* Pierrot in Turquoise *in 1967 and George Underwood painted Pierrot with an elderly woman on the cover of his second album, which was mirrored in a scene in the "Ashes to Ashes" video.*

Carlos Alomar

Guitarist and producer Carlos Alomar has performed alongside a host of rock stars, from Paul McCartney to Bruce Springsteen – and, of course, David Bowie. After playing on 1975's Young Americans, *Alomar went on to record with Bowie – and tour globally as his music director – for the next three decades.*

Let's go back and think not who we are but who we were. So I was in my early twenties; David was in his late twenties. He came to America to do some work with Lulu. I knew Lulu because of *To Sir, with Love* – she was a movie star who was a blue-eyed soul singer and I thought she was amazing. I met Bowie not doing *Young Americans* but as a studio guitarist at RCA studio where he was a producer for Lulu. He didn't know who I was, I didn't know who he was. I didn't know anything about Spiders from Mars. In my formative years, I was listening to Motown, he was listening to R&B – he was listening to blues, you know, Screamin' Jay Hawkins or whoever's records he could get his hands on.

In Britain at that time, if you could get your hands on American records, that would be the coolest thing ever. And all the British musicians started by hearing American rock 'n' roll and then forming a cover band: the Rolling Stones did it, he did it, they all did it, because that's what we all do first. I was trying to learn how to play the Rolling Stones' "Satisfaction" when I was young.

LA '83 – GREG GORMAN (1983)

Renowned portrait photographer Greg Gorman shot Bowie over three decades.
He is a self-professed fan and loved David's professionalism and "crazy sense of humour".
This image was taken from a shoot in Los Angeles in 1983.

——————

So I was a Puerto Rican with an Afro, working at trying to become the guitar player at RCA studio – Elvis Presley's studio – and he was a Brit listening to R&B music all his life and finally coming to America to be in an American recording studio.

I was already working the whole R&B thing, and it really had nothing to do with any British music whatsoever. I just thought that anybody who had anything to do with Lulu, who in turn had worked with Sidney Poitier – that had to be cool. So I was three degrees of separation from Sidney Poitier!

When I met Bowie, I didn't know who he was. He had orange hair and he was white; I had an Afro and I was black. The first thing I did was say, "Come over to my house, have some food and let's just talk," because he was a curious guy, he was interesting, and he wasn't the usual type of guy that I was used to working with.

Next thing I knew he took me up on the invitation. We got together and he started asking me about the Chitlin' Circuit – the same thing happened with Paul McCartney, they wanted to know what it's like to be a rhythm-and-blues guitar player while you're on the road. They wanted to know what the Apollo Theater was like; they wanted to know, "what's the black experience?".

I wanted to know, what the hell is Spiders from Mars? What is the Beatles? So, as musicians do, you exchange road tales. And that's what told me, I feel this guy's background.

That's the communication musicians have. First we meet in the studio, and we play together and we jam together, and it's real cool: "Man, that guy really jams real good, he really plays well." But then you get to know the guy.

Why? Because let's assume they play well, and probably everybody does, or else you wouldn't even be in that room – but do you want to go on the road with him? Because you're gonna probably be with him for a long time. And so if you're a dud or dull or got bad personal hygiene, you're not going anywhere!

At the time I was already married to Robin Clark, who would also end up singing with David; I was already an established musician. Robin Clark was working with the Rascals and Kiss and all that stuff. So we were two individuals who were already established in the music industry in America. We both came from the Apollo Theater; we both had our history. We were not unknown people with no credits: we were formidable New York session musicians. Robin was already doing jingles, background sessions, track work; we were already in the mix, you know, we did not need to be discovered. This was our home town, this was our turf.

David was very curious about the Apollo Theater, where Robin and I spent my early years. And so the fact that we would have people like Cannonball Adderley come down to our rehearsals, the fact that we would have Flip Wilson come down... These were stories he was interested to hear.

We would have dancing lessons, microphone lessons; we would write songs, we would perform these songs. It's kind of like the movie *Fame*.

I relayed these stories to David, so it was like he's backstage at the Apollo. And then I invited him to come down to the Apollo. "Hell, yeah!" Let's go to the Hunts Point Palace to see the Latin band. "Oh, hell, yeah!" I mean, who says no?

And so this is well before I got asked to do *Young Americans*. We kind of bonded as musicians, just hanging out and having a good time. I wasn't asking him for nothing; he wasn't asking me for nothing. It was just cool like that.

———

There was a certain methodology with David, and, that was, if you want to change the sound, well, why don't you change the band?

I mean, we laugh and we might say, "Hmm, in hindsight, damn, that's so logical and easy." Yeah, and that's what he did. Young Americans is the ultimate example of how that worked.

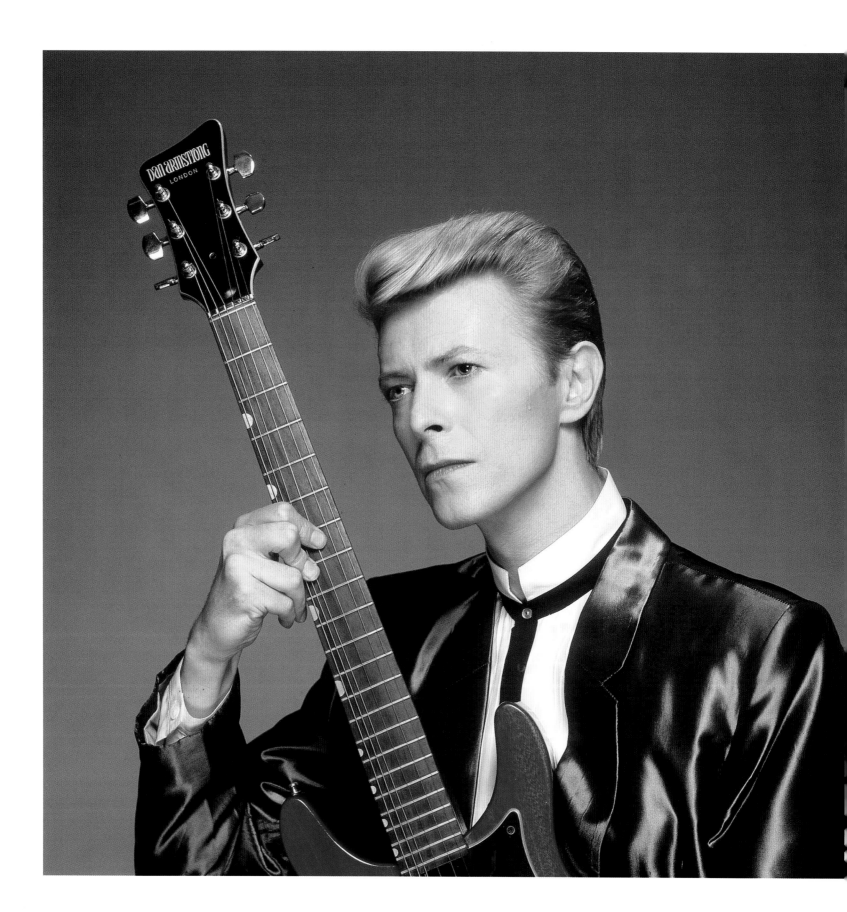

And, yes, Bowie controlled all of that. Because if you're going to look at a concept album then you know exactly what the components have to be in order for you to do that... *Ziggy Stardust and the Spiders from Mars* had a sound that only a four-piece rock band can give you. Can you imagine background singers and a horn section in the Spiders from Mars band? Hell, no.

Let's use the example of "Fame". My riff in that song was actually from our cover of an old song called "Footstompin" – you can see us doing it in footage of the Dick Cavett show online. We had done it on tour, and it was pretty good live. Some things that feel good on tour, just don't work in the studio, and if you're not going to do a song better than the original, don't do it. Because it would just be a cheap imitation of something that just fell flat.

So recording it in the studio didn't really work and the issue became: how can we salvage it? And so, when I came in, the song had already been stripped down to just the drums and the bass and basically it was just blues. What we call one-four-five, the first, the fourth to the fifth chord of the progression. And that was it, it could have been a great blues song.

But then the issue became, what is the particular sound that each musician brings? If a guitar player like Fripp was there, it would have had different components. I happen to like funky stuff and I'd come from that James Brown school of three guitar players locked perfectly in a perfect rhythm; so instead of playing one part with everything in it, I just broke up all my little ideas into being those three James Brown guitar players. So that's what you hear on that track.

SELF ASSIGNMENT – GREG GORMAN (1984)

On of the most striking pictures ever taken of Bowie – by Greg Gorman for Self Assignment *magazine in January 1984.*

I knew David loved all that funk stuff. And he'd asked me so many questions about James Brown and about the Chitlin' Circuit and about black music – I knew there was a reason. With me, if you throw down a challenge and you say lay something down, I'm going to lay it down hard. I was courageous and I just laid down what I thought was good. And he comes in and he says, "Damn, that's funky, that's it. The song is done…let me just put this one guitar part down…and that's it." And there's a certain mystery to "Fame", because there's not a lot of parts. It's just very mysterious and almost creepy and it's got all those little syncopated parts, and that's what made it funky. And David gave me a writing credit on that song – he was a fair and honest man.

The master puppeteer actually did know what he was doing, and not only can you understand that now, but you see it play out constantly on all those albums. To do an electronica album like he did when he started doing the Berlin Trilogy with Brian Eno requires a perception of the future of music and technology – which was that more is less. Brian Eno is doodling around with some new contraption that he has; next thing you know that morphs into this scrolling, bubbling background, which creates a soundscape where a whole record of that kind of stuff totally makes sense.

When you look at David's background in theatre and conceptualizing visuals with music and all of the things that he had with the dance troupes – when you look at those things from a bird's eye view, and if you look at the big picture, it all makes sense.

———

We had to do something that was a little bit different with *Station to Station*, and we definitely knew that we would never go back to the whole soul thing; so we had to go back to rock 'n' roll. But it wasn't rock 'n' roll as we know it, only because there are a lot of facets to that album.

Man, he let me flex my musical muscle on that album. I worked alone with the rhythm section – me, George Murray on bass and Dennis Davis on drums.

YOUNG AMERICAN (1974)

David performing on the Dick Cavett Show *in December 1974. He performed "1984" and "Young Americans" on the show, but this shot shows David's version of The Flares 1961 hit "Foot Stomping," which featured the guitar lick used on "Fame".*

LET'S DANCE – DENIS O'REGAN (1983)
David in a Hong Kong hotel in December 1983. The two shows at the Hong Kong Coliseum marked the end of The Serious Moonlight concerts, which was Bowie's longest and most successful tour, selling 2.6 million tickets over 96 dates in 15 countries.

So we would have the basic tracks done and there wouldn't be anything else (music) there; we wouldn't have to worry about the guitar players coming in and playing anything, or the keyboard players. That way, when we're working out 6/8 time and things like that, we don't have to explain it to anybody. And then they can come in and hear all the stuff and drop it where they can. It makes life a lot easier. And David can control the song more. Some of the songs were classics. Like "Word on a Wing", or "Wild is the Wind".

But what the hell do they have to do with "Stay" or "Station to Station"? Or "TVC15"? Everybody says *Station to Station* was so experimental and it was such a rock 'n' roll album... and all those accolades are given to it. And you're going to tell me that those accolades are for "Wild is the Wind" and "Word on a Wing"? Isn't that somewhat wrong?

"TVC15" is a very light little song. It's almost like a doo-wop song. "Golden Years" is a classic pop song, "Station to Station" is rock 'n' roll. But "Stay"? "Stay" is a funk song. "Stay" could have been "John, I'm Only Dancing". Because there's a G9 in "Stay"; that's a James Brown chord. G9. What rock 'n' roller plays G9? They don't. Earl Slick – I call him Slicky – plays rock 'n' roll chords. I play 13s and 9s. A rock 'n' roll player would play 7s and major chords and power chords.

When Slicky lays down his stuff over the rhythm section that was there, it makes sense. And that's why the combination of me and Slicky is perfect. Because I can work with the rhythm section but I don't have that gigantic power chords that Slicky can bring to it. But, again, you can't say that *Station to Station* was just experimental rock 'n' roll when you've got songs like "Word on a Wing" and "Wild is the Wind" and "Golden Years". There's the oxymoron that is David Bowie.

———

DAVID AND CARLOS – DAVID PLASTIK (1983)

This shot was taken at Madison Square Garden, New York during the Serious Moonlight tour in July 1983. The tour supported the album Let's Dance, *which was Bowie's most successful with around 11 million copies sold worldwide.*

Of course there were drugs around. Oh my God, when we were doing *Young Americans*, you would have this bag of cocaine right on the music stand, and once my wife went in there and knocked it over. And David was so sweet. He was like, "OK, we'll just get another one." You know what, we're musicians. Look, I was raised at the Apollo Theater, where the junkies would be on the street corner, in that weird dance trying to hold themselves up as they nod out from the drug, and they almost fall and they zoom back up again.

And certain things didn't make sense when you were having a conversation with David, but I didn't care as long as he was doing his music and it had nothing to do with me. And why do you think I invited guys like him over to my house to eat? You can't live on milk! Powdered or liquid, bro!

———

Around the time of *Low* was a very strange period for both of us. When David was trying to reignite Iggy Pop's career, he asked me to help him. I went on tour with Iggy, just like David. And so we really started working on this whole trying-to-get-away-from-everything with Iggy in the two albums: *Lust for Life* and *The Idiot*.

Then when David started getting into the whole Berlin thing, it was just an extension of again trying to step away from himself. There's a lot of frustration involved in the period when an artist transitions from one company to another and they're trying to accept, "Dammit, I'm broke, and I still have to sustain myself by touring. Where am I getting the money from?" As far as I know, when David went to Berlin he didn't go to some little, cheap house because he wanted to. It was all he could afford.

People hear about an artist and how he suffers, and people hear them translate their suffering – they're the spokesman for their own pain. And yet their audience never takes it into consideration. It's just something that's in the back of their mind, like, "Oh yeah, Billie Holiday did drugs, but, boy, she sure could sing." You don't even think about the fact that she was a junkie, although you know it. But the attitude is: I don't care what you gotta do, give me that album. And that's sad. And so in that sadness you gotta sometimes step away from yourself, and him and Iggy were in that same place.

———

People often forget about the humanity – they think Bowie was always a superstar and an artist, forgetting there's a person behind it all. And they think wrong. How are you going to write a song called "Weeping Wall", "Art Decade"? Isn't he trying to tell you something with songs like "Be My Wife", "A New Career in a New Town"? But they don't think about that.

It was a transitional time. David was going through a lot of stuff. Times like that are tough: you're trying to get away from your manager; OK, you got away from your manager, but now you realize in paying him off and in paying everyone else off so you could be clean, you're broke. Great. You're now having your marriage come at you, and it's just so confusing. You're trying to work things out but it's all crashing.

But you need a new album and the record company's changed, and you gotta give them what they want.

Records during these days had an A- and a B-side. Everybody puts everything on the A-side, don't they? When was the last time you took your album and flipped it over on the B-side? And yet when you have an album that the company wants, you give them an A-side like on *Low*, where you have "Speed of Life", "Breaking Glass", "What in the World" and these songs that everybody's singing. And then when you turn it over on the B-side, well, you might as well turn off the lights, because you just went into subterranea and you just went into a soundscape, into a sci-fi movie. And there are no words.

Why? Because a musician understands that the integrity of your music is based on the emotional attachment that you have to that. If I'm weeping and I'm feeling bad and

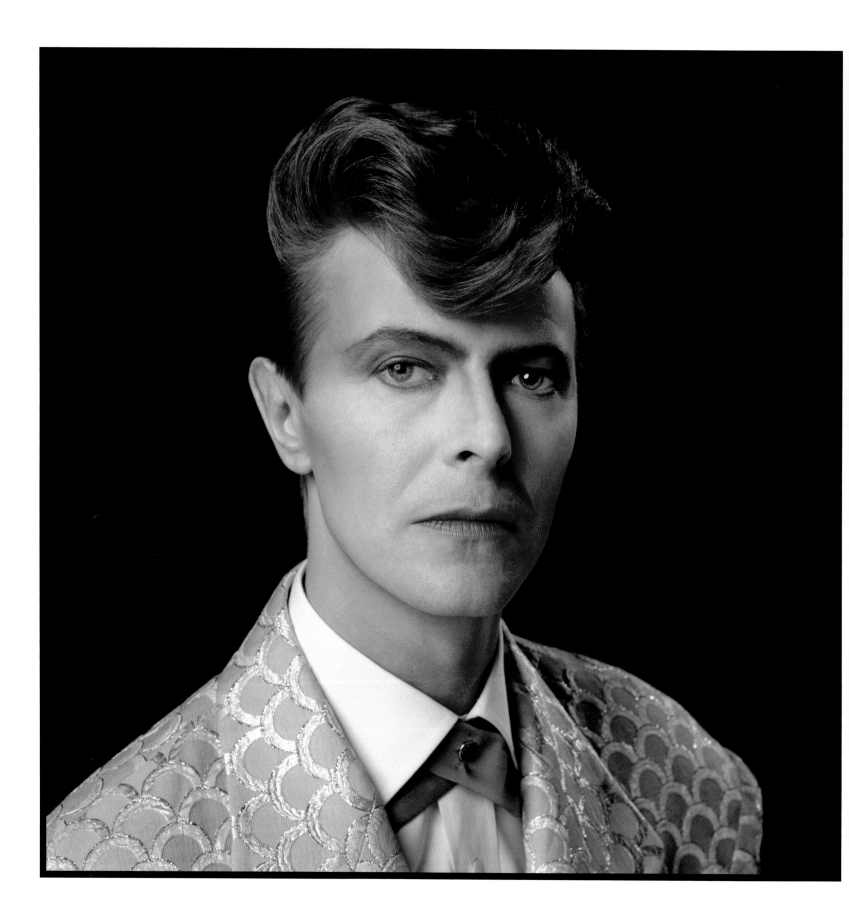

you hear a song called "Weeping Wall", you can hear the lament. You can hear the tears. You can hear it in there, you know what I mean? So why not give them the A-side that they want, but the B-side is all yours?

———

Brian Eno changed me for ever because he asked me to clean the palette and to start out with new paint. I can do painting fine, but now you're asking me to go into watercolours? They bleed everywhere, and I'm uncomfortable, and because I'm uncomfortable I resist. But then I realize that as the colours bleed they form these images on their own. All I gotta do is try not to stop them and see what happens when the colours just bleed. And then I realize what I'm seeing is not the colours, what I'm seeing is in the space of white that is not coloured, in between the colours. And what I'm doing is painting the spaces.

During the Eighties it was a little better, because we were going into *Scary Monsters* and *Lodger* and things like that. It was a period where his home life and his music were at least controllable. I think under those circumstances that's a pretty good thing, because you want to have a settled life. During that time Bowie also moved in next door to me. We were living on 26th Street. He had the east wing and I had the west wing. And this was a real fantastic time for us because, like the way we started, it allowed both of us to just be people. And then it was winter time and Lennon got shot, and it just was so shitty. But we were together, and so it gave us a period where

———

FAME, FASHION, PHOTOGRAPHY – CHALKIE DAVIES (1986)
This shot was taken on the set of Labyrinth *in 1986 by Chalkie Davies. A print was made for Cancer Research UK in 2016.*

we could kind of mourn and talk, and I was just glad to be able to be there during that time.

I didn't know too much about Bowie's life as a father, because he kept all of that stuff to himself... Little Zowie was always little Zowie for me; we met him when he was such a little boy and I remember once when we were in the Château d'Hérouville, he was like, "Please don't forget me", and I said, "I'll never forget you." And then we found out he doesn't want to be called Zowie and he wasn't called Zowie any more. Much later, we had already been watching some of the films he directed when we suddenly realized, oh my God, Duncan Jones is actually Zowie. Which was kind of cool. But I'm glad that David kept his private life to himself.

———

I saw David at Tony Visconti's birthday party last year, and he was very, very fragile. In hindsight, I can see what was happening. He came by with his friend of many years, Corinne Schwab, and it was just nice to have Corinne, David, Robin and I together again. We talked about old times, and it was good to talk about things, heal old wounds, reminisce and just enjoy our time together. And now I know why we were together again. Now I understand it was that goodbye, you know?

It was a moment just to celebrate and just be glad to be together. When things like that happen, you just take the moment as the moment is. But, in hindsight, when you look at the overall picture and you get the bird's-eye view, you realize that it was a goodbye. It was that iconic moment when you're able to see a friend and say goodbye but not in a mournful way. Just, I'll talk to you later, and not have it be so damn morbid.

Part of what made David so special was that he was a listener and he was curious. All great science, all great scientists, all great people like that, I think that they never outgrow their childhood. A child is fearless in that he wants to know what's around the corner, he wants to touch that hot stove, he wants to know why is that fire so bright? He knows he's going to get burned but you can't tell a kid not to turn that corner.

Debbie Harry & Chris Stein

Debbie Harry and Chris Stein co-founded the groundbreaking new wave group Blondie, which still plays live and records. They were lynchpins of the New York scene that David Bowie became fascinated with in the late Seventies. After Bowie and Iggy Pop heard Blondie's self-titled debut album, they gave Blondie a major opportunity – the opening slot on the North American leg of Iggy's 1977 Idiot World tour, which also gave Stein, a skilled photographer, a chance to shoot some memorable backstage photos. (Bowie produced and co-wrote The Idiot, *Iggy's March 1977 album, and served as keyboardist on the tour – he also worked on the follow-up LP,* Lust for Life.*)*

Harry and Stein shared their recollections of Bowie in a joint interview for this book.

Before you met Bowie, what impact did he and his music have on you?

Chris Stein: We were fans, you know?

Debbie Harry: The first time he came to New York, and played Carnegie Hall, that was a big moment.

C: It was pretty soon after the *Ziggy* album. I remember he did a lot of acoustic stuff. It was great, it was awesome, it was big. One of those shows you'll never forget. It was a big event for everybody in the downtown music scene, too. It was more than just music, there was a social aspect. People came together around him, I think.

———

ABSOLUTE BEGINNERS – CHALKIE DAVIES (1986)

This is the cover shot for the single "Absolute Beginners," which was the theme tune to the film of the same name that was released in 1986. The film – directed by Julien Temple, who had worked on the "Jazzin' for Blue Jean" video – wasn't received well by the critics or film goers, but the song faired much better reaching number 2 in the UK charts. The session musicians who worked on the song (including Rick Wakeman on keyboards) received an invite to the studio on a card from a "Mr X". When they arrived at Abbey Road studios they discovered it was Bowie.

Lou Reed, Andy Warhol, and a theater full of kids in their best glam regalia were also in the audience for that 8th November, 1972 show, one of the most important of Bowie's career – which included a cover of "Waiting for the Man" by Reed's band the Velvet Underground. The decadent after-party that night in Bowie's hotel suite inspired the lyrics of the Aladdin Sane track "Watch That Man," which Bowie was already performing live when he returned to New York for dates at Radio City Music Hall three months later.

D: Everybody wanted to meet him; everybody wanted to hang out. Unlike some people he was 100 per cent cool with the downtown music scene. He wasn't someone who was outmoded, he was someone who represented something that we could get behind.

C: He was always reinventing and experimenting with these different styles, so that was also an important model for us. He was always so very eclectic.

D: He really was a great performer, and he was into theatrics, it really was part of what all of us aspired to do. He was urban, you know?

C: He had that whole attraction to Andy Warhol, because he was, in many ways, doing what Andy did in the music world. Bowie was the kingpin behind this whole scene that revolved around him. Like Andy Warhol, Bowie was someone who everyone, everything, always had some connection to, you know? In New York, everybody had a connection to Andy, once or twice removed. It was the same with Bowie.

Blondie played 24 dates with Iggy Pop and Bowie on the Idiot World tour, in March and April of 1977. For their first date, in Montreal, they drove their van straight to Canada overnight after a show at New York's Max's Kansas City.

How did you end up on the Idiot World tour?

D: They chose us: I think they asked a couple of different bands, and we were top of the list.

DEBBIE AND DAVID – CHRIS STEIN (1977)

*David and Debbie are shown here backstage at The Palladium, New York in March, 1977
during Iggy Pop's The Idiot tour. The tour consisted of 29 performances in three countries
(UK, Canada and US). Blondie supported Iggy on the Canadian and US dates,
taking over from punk band The Vibrators who played the US gigs.*

C: It was pretty phenomenal, what Bowie did for Iggy on that tour. Everybody was aware of what was going on with that. It was a great moment.

D: Bowie had just released that *Low* album, and I don't think it was what the critics really expected. The whole situation spoke to his totality as an artist. That he would have this *Low* album out and then he would take a back seat on stage and tour with Iggy. It's the same kind of thing he showed us with this last album, *Blackstar* – that his visualization of his art was his life. It wasn't at all superficial or commercial; he really was deeply involved with the things that he did. There was a totality to his presentations.

C: He was really intrigued by the punk and new-wave scene, and wanted to connect with that. When we talked to him, he really wanted to know about the scene and what was going on in New York and other bands. I really remember talking a lot about Tom Verlaine's hairdo with him. Several times.

Did he give you any suggestions or advice?

C: He told Debbie stuff about working the stage, about approaching her performances almost as an actor.

D: I would call it technical advice.

Did you get any insights on what that time was about for David? Why he was out there playing keyboards for Iggy Pop instead of on a big David Bowie tour?

C: I think he wanted to connect with this other aspect of the music reality of the time. I think he appreciated who Iggy was, certainly, and wanted to be a part of that. Midway through the tour, we played two shows in Detroit, and it was just a crazy hometown crowd for Iggy. People went completely nuts for him.

Did David seem to be enjoying himself over there on the keyboards, or did it seem like he wanted to get back in the spotlight?

C: I think he liked it. He was really loud, he had this Leslie [speaker] off stage, you know,

BLONDIE TRIBUTE – CHRIS STEIN (2016)

Chris and Debbie during rehearsals for The Music of David Bowie concerts held at Carnegie Hall, New York on 1st April, 2016. The evening had been planned before David's death and turned into a memorial concert after the news broke. Debbie sang "Starman" at the show.

fucking superloud. The band was great. It was a terrific band with those guys, it was very simple, and it was basic, but it was really cool. People were throwing leather jackets and cameras on stage at Iggy; it was crazy.

D: And underwear.

C: And underwear, yeah, it's traditional.

D: Those girls, you know, in the front row…

What do you remember about the pictures that Chris took on tour?

C: In addition to the ones with Debbie and David, there's also a whole bunch of pictures I shot with Debbie and Iggy, I don't think it was the same day, but Iggy was much more relaxed than David when I shot him. David was more careful about what his image was, what he put out. I don't think he knew about my photographic skills, so it's a little snapshotty for me; I would have liked to have done something a little bit more set up. The stuff I did with Iggy was very cool.

And after that tour, what personal contact did you have with Bowie?

C: Over the years we would go out a bunch of times, and you know, we'd see him around. Not a lot. We hung out with him more in that period of the Seventies, I think, than later. We had this fancy place on the Upper East Side briefly, and he showed in the middle of the night one time with Mick Jagger: that was a great moment, actually.

Because he's no longer with us, sad as that is, we now have the opportunity of looking at his entire career from start to finish. How would you sum up what Bowie achieved?

D: The thing that was interesting for me was that he was always discovering things and looking: he was an enquiring kind of person. As I said earlier, there was a totality to his thought process and what he ended up coming out with for himself. He travelled a lot, of course, because he was on the road, and the influences of different cultures around the world came through. As a solo artist I really sort of envy him, being able to embrace these different characterizations and bring them to life for himself. He made these transitions and people accepted them. I don't think there was ever a moment when somebody said, "Ew, we don't like that. Have you seen what Bowie's doing now?!"

C: The sense I get from him was he was always striving, maybe kind of never really satisfied; he was just always trying to move ahead.

D: If you look at the idea of what a rock 'n' roll star or a rock 'n' roll artist is, Bowie was a classic. He sort of approached things as if he were a classical musician or a composer or a fine artist. You know, just as Picasso had periods, I think that you can clearly see the same thing with Bowie. He really had a sort of classical mind.

Martyn Ware

Founding member of the Human League and Heaven 17, Martyn Ware is known today for his work as a composer, producer and music programmer, including the creation of sound installations. Alongside composer and filmmaker Alexis Kirke, he produced data sonifications of David Bowie's albums for the V&A exhibition, Bowie Is.

Right through my career Bowie has been an enormous influence. It all started in the early Seventies when I was 16 and I first started going out. Phil Oakey was my best mate then so we used to go to things like the early Roxy Music concerts and went to see *Ziggy Stardust* at City Hall in Sheffield. Actually, we were a bit naughty and we broke in because we couldn't afford it. I was always an obsessive Bowie fan, right back to the *Space Oddity* album. *The Man who Sold the World* was a hugely popular track at the all-night parties we used to have at Phil Oakey's house. We used to have an eight-track cartridge player with it on. It was quite unique at the time because you could have something play endlessly, and we used to put either that on or *Ziggy Stardust*, *Space Oddity* or *Hunky Dory*, actually, and kinda let them play all night while we were going to sleep.

I think it's safe to say that the little blue touchpaper for me were the two albums *Low* and *"Heroes"*, particularly *Low*, which made me think I really, really wanted to do that.

"DAVID BOWIE" – JOHN BELLANY (1987)

Bowie was a collector of the acclaimed Scottish artist John Bellany and owned 15 of his paintings. He befriended the painter and made visits to Port Seton, Bellany's birth place. He once told the painter he thought one work "stood up well" to the Tintoretto it hung next to in his Swiss home.

And around the same time Kraftwerk's *Trans-Europe Express* came out. This was a critical moment for me, thinking this is something I really wanted to have a go at – even though I did not have any equipment.

Low was like nothing else, but it still had elements of rock-pop music. Lyrically, it was more like an art inspiration, for me, like conceptual art. And then, of course, on the second side you had "Warszawa", and the idea of having an album that just dissolved into pure sonic imagery really: it all came back to prog rock, which was something I loved as well, but in a much more futuristic sense. I've always believed that popular music at its best paints vivid images in the mind; that each individual paints their own images different from everybody else's. And Bowie had that capability, leaving enough wiggle room in his work that you can populate it with your own meaning and artistic sensibility.

Obviously, with those two albums there was a sense that, to use a cliché, they were ahead of their time. It was kind of a hint at what was coming, it was a hint at synth-pop and new wave. He was starting to embody some of that, especially with help from Eno.

It's funny, the American perspective of new wave: if you look at it as a Venn diagram, new wave incorporated a lot of the creative and credible end of the post-punk scene. There wasn't really the same kind of terminology in Britain about this sort of thing. Post punk didn't really exist in Britain. There was a golden era of around 1980 to '84 when the scene was highly creative in Britain, but then it kind of became very commandeered by common marketing people and lost its vibe. It was really abroad that they appreciated it as new wave, and yet a lot of it was coming from Britain.

I can only speak for myself, but in the early Human League and early Heaven 17 we always regarded what we did as an artistic enterprise, primarily. It's nice to be successful and appreciated by the general public, but that was more pushed on to us by the record company's need for a return on their investment. We've always regarded what we do as art. It's terribly unfashionable now but that's just the way it is.

HUMAN LEAGUE (1979)

Human League, from left to right: Adrian Wright, Ian Craig Marsh, Philip Oakey and Martyn Ware.

Bowie's pushing of the boundaries of rock in the Seventies very much influenced me at that time. The key component in doing what we did, initially, was this brave new world of the portable synthesizers. It just coincided with when we wanted to do music like that, and when we had enough money to do it. We just saw this as a blank canvas, really; we saw it as the wild frontier of music. In our youthful arrogance we used to think that rock 'n' roll was dying, and punk was just yet another manifestation of rock 'n' roll, which it was, in fact. But actually what was more impressive and important was the more creative stuff that came in the post-punk period, or new wave as Americans would call it, which was much more important and impressive than punk itself as far as I was concerned.

———

I met Bowie in '78 when he came to see Human League. I have a photo of it, amazingly – I couldn't believe someone took a photo of it. It was completely unannounced; we had no inkling he was coming, he and his entourage. I only found out recently that a month before, he and Iggy Pop had tried to get into one of our gigs at the Marquee Club in Wardour Street, Soho. But they turned up too late and it was full, and the stupid bouncer wouldn't let them in. Fortunately, David was patient and came to see us again in this real shithole of a pub down in Fulham. The dressing room, to give you an idea, was like a cubbyhole, really; the ceiling and the floor were covered in graffiti. It had no door and, like all those places, it just smelled of beer and pee.

———

PORTRAIT – CLIVE ARROWSMITH (1977)

This shot comes from a photo session in London with the photographer Clive Arrowsmith.
Clive had shot David before in 1968 when he was part of a performance trio called the Feathers.
Clive also shot the cover of Mick Ronson's second album Play Don't Worry.

For me, it was like Jesus stepping out of a medieval painting and walking into your front room. It was just bizarre, I couldn't comprehend it; I still can't quite comprehend it to this day, really. He was such a hero. And then, of course, no pressure at all, that was 10 minutes before we were due to go on stage.

Bowie described us in the press as the future of music, which was immensely flattering, but it was quite a while before all that translated into sales, unfortunately. That's why ultimately, I suppose, the split happened, because there was such external pressure being put on us by the record company and behind our backs through our management to get two bands for the price of one.

Ultimately, Bowie was a conceptual artist. It just so happens that the media he used were rock 'n' roll, identity, the way he dressed – he even did theatre and film, of course. The way that he approached his work, it was like using an album as a medium to paint on, that's how I saw it anyway. It was like every new album was a new exhibition of his core philosophy, artistic philosophy as manifest within the framework of rock.

To me, there's a clarity and purity to the albums he made until round about *Lodger,* and then, he started to get a little dissolute. It started to kind of all fall apart a little bit, even though he was still ridiculously talented. Not that the albums were worse, but they were less focused somehow; they seemed to have more diversity or less of a theme per album, less of a kind of attitude per album. I remember when *Lodger* came out being quite disappointed, initially. Of course it had some classic tracks on it. Bit it felt episodic rather than integrated. I feel that until *Blackstar* it didn't really get any different.

The V&A had a special night for the *David Bowie Is* exhibition, for which they invited myself and a friend of mine, who's a professor at the University of Plymouth, to look at some creative ideas to do with David Bowie as a unique exhibition. So I came up with the idea of datasonifying him, a sonification of the data of his career in sound, in three-dimensional sound. The way it worked was I analyzed all his albums. I had a theory that I wanted to test, which was that if you multiplied the percentage of major chords in his songs by the tempo, you could see whether the faster and more cheerful songs

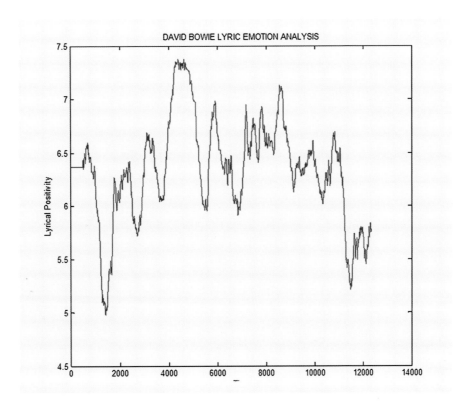

DAVID BOWIE LYRIC EMOTION ANALYSIS

EMOTIONAL ANALYSIS (2013)

Running from "The Laughing Gnome" through to "Tin Machine" Martyn Ware and composer Alexis Kirke analyzed the emotional content of Bowie's output by using a database of emotionally-annotated words, which were given scores based on their emotional positivity and their physical intensity. It shows that Bowie's music becomes emotionally more positive from the start up to "Let's Dance" and afterwards becomes more erratic.

were more saleable. So to see if there was a correlation there we created this coefficient and analyzed all the songs, and that took a while but it was fun. And, lo and behold, the correlation was very strong until *Let's Dance* , when it started diverging. In other words, he started trying too hard and the sales didn't follow him – as I saw it – trying to be more commercial.

Until and including *Let's Dance*, the number of faster tracks and the more major-chord-heavy tracks directly correlated to the amount of sales of his albums. After that he tried faster tracks and more major chords in his tracks but the sales started declining. Now there are various factors involved in that. It's hard to beat the sales of an album like *Let's Dance* anyway, but it was a pretty consistent decline from that point. It's an interesting insight into what I regard to be a universally successful career, creatively. Possibly because of the amount of money he was drawing in from the record company, he became obsessed with selling records around about that time. It's interesting because that pedal-to-the-metal thing only works for a short period of time and then the law of diminution returns.

Blackstar was an immensely powerful work: almost like the final reorientating of his work towards a purely artistic purpose. He had nothing to lose at that time: he knew he was dying. I don't think he really cared whether it sold or not, or what the critics thought, it's way beyond that. And I've got admiration for him from that perspective. While I didn't necessarily like all the tracks on the album, I love the artistic authenticity of it.

———

In terms of rock stars in this century and the last, I rate him at the top. I think his output is better than the Beatles and people like the Rolling Stones. Of course, it's like comparing chalk and cheese, but he's number one for me. It's the innovation and the diversity of what he did and the incalculable influence he's had on artists, in particular recording artists, which has not been really acknowledged properly yet. It was obvious that he affected a lot of people deeply when he passed. But, I can't think of anybody, not even John Lennon, really, who – for his time – has had more influence on more than one generation of musical artists.

In my opinion he did probably his best work before I even started, and I started 35 years ago. The stuff he did became so timeless that it's still influencing people now. Young bands still quote *Hunky Dory*, for instance; it's quite a common one that people regard as a very influential singer–songwriter-type album. And it was a very underrated album. The previous two, *Space Oddity* and *The Man who Sold the World,* are also vastly underrated. From both of those to *Hunky Dory* and *Ziggy Stardust*, I think they're all amazing: lyrically, the complex chord structures, the unique storytelling... There's nothing else like it. The subject matters he covered were unbelievable.

I still listen to those early albums now – and I love the delicacy and the ephemeral nature of his voice, looking back on it, before his voice got set in stone, before it matured and became a fully blown instrument. He was obviously influenced by Dylan, whom I'm not a big fan of, personally, but he was influenced by him, and he was almost like that – singing, talking, talking to you one on one, the listener; some of those early tunes, they speak to you on an intimate level, and I love that. That's what hooked me.

Derek Boshier

British-born, LA-based artist Derek Boshier was pronounced one of the seminal generation of British pop artists after appearing in the Young Contemporaries *exhibition at the Whitechapel Art Gallery, London, 1961. He has produced artwork for a songbook by the Clash, and worked on the cover of David Bowie's* Lodger, *among other Bowie projects.*

In 1979 I was asked by the British Council to curate a show. The idea for it was up to me. I ended up doing a show at The Hayward Gallery called Lives, subtitled *An Exhibition of Artists Whose Work is Based on Other Peoples' Lives.* There were about 24 artists in it, and I tried to include both high art and low art. For instance, David Hockney and Keith Haring were in it, but I also went to the studio of a stamp designer who had designed a beautiful stamp with a bicyclist on it. I told him what I was going to do, and he said, no, I can't be in that exhibition, I'm not an artist. I said, what do you mean you're not an artist? Your work will be seen by millions of people, unlike some of Hockney's and Haring's, because it had been on a stamp. So I persuaded him to be in it.

Another person I put in the show was Brian Duffy, the photographer, who had worked with David a lot. After that first meeting, Duffy contacted me and he said, "Derek, I've got something to tell you. I've got this friend and I think you'd really

---

THE ELEPHANT MAN – DEREK BOSHIER (1980)

Bowie owned a number of acclaimed pop artist Boshier's works, including the full size original of this painting (see page 139). Boshier was responsible for the art direction on the Lodger *album the year before, which features a similarly distorted Bowie face. The Elephant Man was Bowie's first conventional stage performance, which drew on his early mime training to imitate John Merrick's physicality and brought rave reviews throughout its tour of the US in 1980.*

get on." And the way he phrased it I thought it was a blind date. I thought the friend was female. I went to Duffy's studio, and of course it was David. In retrospect I might have anticipated it, because about two weeks earlier I'd been in an art bookshop in Covent Garden and the owner recognized me and asked if I knew David Bowie. And I said, "Well, I know of him." He said, "He's been in here a couple of times asking for your catalogues." So that's how I first met David.

We had some meetings and Duffy thought up the way of doing the cover for *Lodger*. We shot it from above; we cut the table to get the shot. It went on for several weeks, I think, and then I had a phone call from David. He said, "We need to knock this record cover on the head and get it out... Can you have it ready on Thursday?" So I said, "Thursday's fine – is there any chance of meeting in the daytime?" He said, "Great, come to Berlin for lunch." Yeah, he was a rock star. In this same conversation I said, "Oh, David, we haven't talked about the inside art." He said, "Do what you like." So, I picked things: life, death, Che Guevara's autopsy in Bolivia, Mantegna the Renaissance painter's *Death of Christ*, which is in Milan Cathedral, the image of David being shot... A photography student of mine at the Royal College was doing a whole essay on mortuaries, I used that. And then I used a knitting pattern for babies and young children. And two wristwatches, which seemed to fascinate people. One guy wrote me an email and asked why I used those particular watches.

———

David was such a fucking interesting guy: any conversation with him was interesting. His PR, whom he was going out with at the time, said, "You know, guys, I totally understand David, I'm his chief PR person, but when you two get together I sometimes can't understand your conversation because you're talking English phraseology and jokes and stuff, this whole cultural thing." Well, David and I did have a few things in common. I actually studied a little bit of mime, too, when I was at the Royal College of Art. David obviously uses it in his productions and I use it in paintings. And we had this other link, which had to do with the falling-figure motif. He did *The Man who Fell to Earth* and I did lots of paintings of falling figures. So we had the falling figure in common. I guess the working-class background was a shared thing, too. Unlike some celebrities, he used his fame well. He was interested in everything, always creative. For instance, the session where we did Lodger, I was early, and I know that the make-up artist wasn't there when I first arrived. And the first thing I noticed about David was that he had a bandage on his hand. I said, "Oh, David, what did you do?" And he said, "I fucking burned my hand on the coffee maker this morning."

We were sitting, and chatting, and David was looking in the mirror and combing his hair, and he had this bandage on and in came the make-up guy. He was a great guy – he was the make-up guy for Michael Jackson, Liz Taylor... When he saw David's hand he said, "Oh, David, that'll be an hour or so." And David said, "No, leave it." That's typical David – just go with the moment. And that's an extra thing, I think, that's an extra intrigue to him. And it's typical David to turn something like that into a positive.

David was always an incredibly generous person. I remember one story his PR told me. We were talking about art and she said, "David is so interested in art. He often goes to final-degree shows at art schools. He went to one in London and he was looking around, and he saw the work of a young photographer, just finishing college. 'You know these are interesting photographs,' he said, 'just take his details.' So within two weeks, his PR went to David and said, 'Oh, by the way, Italian *Vogue* want to do a thing on you – you OK with that, what do you think?' David said, 'Tell you what, one condition, tell them I want them to use that photographer.'"

So that fucking photographer, his first job is to photograph David Bowie for Italian *Vogue*. And he's put things my way like that all the time. One time he was doing an interview with the Village Voice and at the end, apropos of actually nothing, he just dropped my name, quoted me on something. He says, "and I think Derek Boshier was right when he said..." Whatever it was I'd said. He did that kind of thing all the time.

―――

DEREK BOSHIER – TONY EVANS (C.1965)

Pop artist Derek Boshier first came to prominence as a student at the Royal College of Art in London in the early '60s with contemporaries David Hockney, Allen Jones and R. B. Kitaj. He has worked with all kinds of materials and media including installations, film and three dimensional objects and his works range from Pop and Op art, to abstraction and political conceptual art.

I have a Paris gallery. I had this show and my gallery owner did something that he would never do now – it was the first time I ever met him – he actually drove to the airport to pick me up, de Gaulle Airport. So he drove me and he said, "It's good to meet you. You've had some correspondence – there's a guy called Adrian Berg who's writing an essay on one of the French Impressionists, and also this man David Blodgie." And I said, "Who?!" He said, "David Blodgie. I think he's a musician." "Was it David Bowie?" "Oh yeah, Bowie, he kept calling me and asking if he could come to the private view. And I said, 'Are you a friend of Derek's?' and he said yeah. So then he kept calling me again and said, 'Any chance of meeting Derek before the opening?' And I said, 'Yeah, I probably can arrange that.' David called again and I said, 'Look, I'm doing a little buffet at my house, come to that.' And he said, 'Can I bring my wife?' 'Yeah, yeah sure.'"

Then I saw David the day before my show was hung. He came to the gallery, looked around, and after a bit, I started talking about things, and I thought, No, I'll pull back. I said, "David, I'll leave it to you, you just have a look without my interference." So he looked about for half an hour and he came back and said, "Oh, I see you sold two paintings already," and I said, "Yeah," and he said, "Well, you just sold two more." So he bought two. He was my best collector.

———

One of the great things about working with David, and working with the Clash, is that I got a chance to get my work out to a wider audience than the smaller art-world one. I designed some sets for him in '78. They are mostly at my studio, and the V&A Museum bought one of the sets just before the Bowie show, which is still on world tour – it's in that show. David called me and he said, have you ever made any stage sets? I said, yes, I actually have, way back in '68, I designed the sets and the costumes for a production of *The Life of Apollinaire*. He said, "Well, I'm doing a tour, but it's not a stadium one, it's a

big theatre show, and would you like to design the sets?" I said, "What's my brief?" And he said, "I tell you what, think of big bands"– so I'm thinking Duke Ellington – "and then think punk." That was just too wide a brief; I could do anything. There's a man with a guitar flying through the air, a skyscraper in an urban landscape, which I'd actually designed partly from a competition to do a billboard, and I thought, I'll use that again. So that was that.

When I first moved out to Texas, where I lived for 13 years, David got in touch to ask if he could use my image of the Houston skyline projected on his body for the *Let's Dance* cover. It looked fantastic. When I came back to the UK we met up with him and Iman, and we went to Burghclere chapel. So of course my daughters had gone to school and told everyone, "David Bowie's coming to see us." And the other kids didn't believe them at all, and they were very upset. So I said, "David, you know, my two daughters, they're getting such a hell of a time because they told everybody that you were coming." And he said, "Tell them to come over." And he was so good – put his arms around them, and everyone photographed him and then they went back to school with the photo. That was beautiful.

He came to a couple of my openings in Paris. And I said, "Oh, what are you in Paris for?" He said, "To come to your opening, but now that I'm here I'll do a few things." And I said, "Yeah, but..." He said, "No, I came for your opening. But," he said, "now I'm here I'll do a few things." In England, David can walk about the street. In England people were like, "Ello, David, how you doing, all right mate?" France was a very different story.

MUSTIQUE – DERRY MOORE (1992)

Shot for an interview with Architectural Digest, *Bowie is seen reclining with his sax in his Balinese-style house on the Island of Mustique. He bought the land in 1986 after being stranded following a party at Mick Jagger's house on the island. Bowie later sold the villa to publisher Felix Dennis.*

I was having coffee with my gallery dealer in a café where all the curators and a lot of artists used to hang out. There was a French gallery owner, and he asked me what I'd been to see, and if I'd done the tourist things. I said no, I'm never really a tourist here, I usually just hang out in the Marais and I walk to the Louvre. But, I said, you know what I'd like to see? That big Matisse show called *Henry Matisse: The Early Years in Nice*, but it has such long queues to get in. So the gallery owner calls over the café and he says, Jacques! This English artist here wants to get into the exhibition – you're the fucking curator. And he said, oh yeah, come early tomorrow, we don't open till 12. My dealer asked if he could come too, which the guy was fine with, and I said, is there any possibility of two more people coming? The day before David had said, "Oh, I would like to go to that Matisse show," but he'd just get mobbed, so he couldn't. The guy said, OK, who is it? And I said, well, it's David Bowie and his wife.

So we arranged to meet for coffee in the morning about 10.30. And then we'd just walk to the gallery, and the curator told us to go into the back door. So the time came, and we started towards this side-door entrance, and there were, like, 150 high-school students. All of a sudden someone said: "Bowie!" I get hold of David and we're fighting people off and we're pushing him through the door. It was that level of hysteria.

Anyhow, I'm not an art historian but I know a bit about art and I like Matisse, so I take David round. The gallery wasn't open to the public for an hour and a half, but we go into this one gallery, and there's 30 high-school students looking at a painting with their teacher teaching them; David Bowie walks past, and 30 heads follow him, like an audience at a tennis match in slow motion.

———

The story behind the portrait on page 131 is this: I'm in New York and it's August 1980. Fucking hot. I enter the loft studio I'm renting, and I get a phone call from David. "Hi, Derek, do you still want to do that portrait of me?" I said, sure. He said, "Well, I'm in

New York; I'm rehearsing for *The Elephant Man* Off-Broadway." So we fixed up a time for him to come. The studio I rented was on the Bowery. And David actually stepped over a body to press the door bell. He was dressed in this immaculate white shirt, which was freshly laundered, and red trousers, red socks and red shoes. I didn't know how long I'd have him for, but he was there for three and a half hours all together in the end. I didn't know how long it would take so I thought of doing a portrait just of his head, those eyes, small pupils.

So that was that, and then we got talking about *The Elephant Man*, and I asked how rehearsals were going. He said, it's all right, but sometimes I have to stay on stage for five minutes at a time like this, and he did this pose, a distorted face, and I thought, Well, fuck, that's the portrait. Just the head. Not the glamorous David, I'll do the other one. So that's what I did. And then I had a flash of a famous Manet painting called *Le fifre*. It's of a young boy, bright-red trousers, playing a flute. David's pose echoed that, so that's what I did. And I did another portrait of him. I did a show at the National Portrait Gallery about two years ago and I had one of my Bowie portraits in there, one I still own, a head.

David sent me an email a few weeks before he died. He said: "I just got to write you, Derek, and tell you I thought your new book was so good." I had lost contact several years before that, when he had that heart attack. I wasn't worried about him because I kept reading about him in music magazines and everywhere.

So many celebrities, they're not celebrities for nothing. They have what it takes to be a celebrity. And David certainly did. I was with David once, and, again, I remember sitting in front of a mirror with him; we were chatting, and there was one of those actor's make-up mirrors with naked light bulbs all around them. As we were chatting the PR person came over and said, "David, there's a photographer here from *Paris Match*." David, in real life, used to always walk quite slowly and talk quietly, he never shouted, different from the almost narcissistic public persona. He goes to the photographer and says, "Are you ready to go?" And the photographer said "Yeah," so they start shooting, and he became David Bowie. And then straight after he said, "Let's go sit down again."

It was like watching Clark Kent going into the telephone booth and becoming Superman, then turning back. He was like that. And I always tell people that we think we know what we look like, and we know each other by looking in the mirror and photographs and films, but David knew what he looked like from every angle, from the back of his head even. He knew every part.

BLACK TIE, WHITE NOISE – ANTON CORBIJN (1993)
Shot by acclaimed photographer and director Anton Corbijn, this picture comes from a shoot for Max *magazine in March 1993 ahead of the release of* Black Tie, White Noise *the following month. The album marked Bowie's return as a solo artist following the two Tin Machine albums. The record was received well by critics and debuted at No. 1 in the UK album charts.*

Nile Rodgers

Superstar producer, guitarist, composer and arranger Nile Rodgers has been a key force in shaping popular music through the past four decades, as co-founder of Chic, a hitmaking producer to artists including David Bowie, Duran Duran, and Madonna, and, most recently, a session guitarist with Daft Punk and Disclosure.

David made it clear he wanted me to make him a commercial record instantly. Instantly. When I say instantly, here's exactly how long it took to get into the studio to do *Let's Dance*: I meet him for the first time between four and six in the morning at the Continental after-hours club. He called my house a few days later. I don't remember giving him my phone number but I must have: he called my house repeatedly, but I was having my house renovated, and the guys who were working there kept hanging up on him.

"Hey, Mr Rodgers, there's some fucking guy calling up saying he's David Bowie! What do you want us to do?"

I said, "ARGH! Next time he calls, give me the phone!" I said, "That IS David Bowie."

"Oh, hey, sorry, OK."

So he called me up, we talked, and we decided that we would meet at the Carlyle Hotel. That was so awesome that I told my girlfriend that I'm meeting David there.

OUTSIDE – KEVIN CUMMINS (1995)

This photo was taken in November 1995 by music photographer Kevin Cummins. The shoot took place in East London when Bowie had been rehearsing ahead of his four shows at Wembley Arena as part of the Outside *tour.*

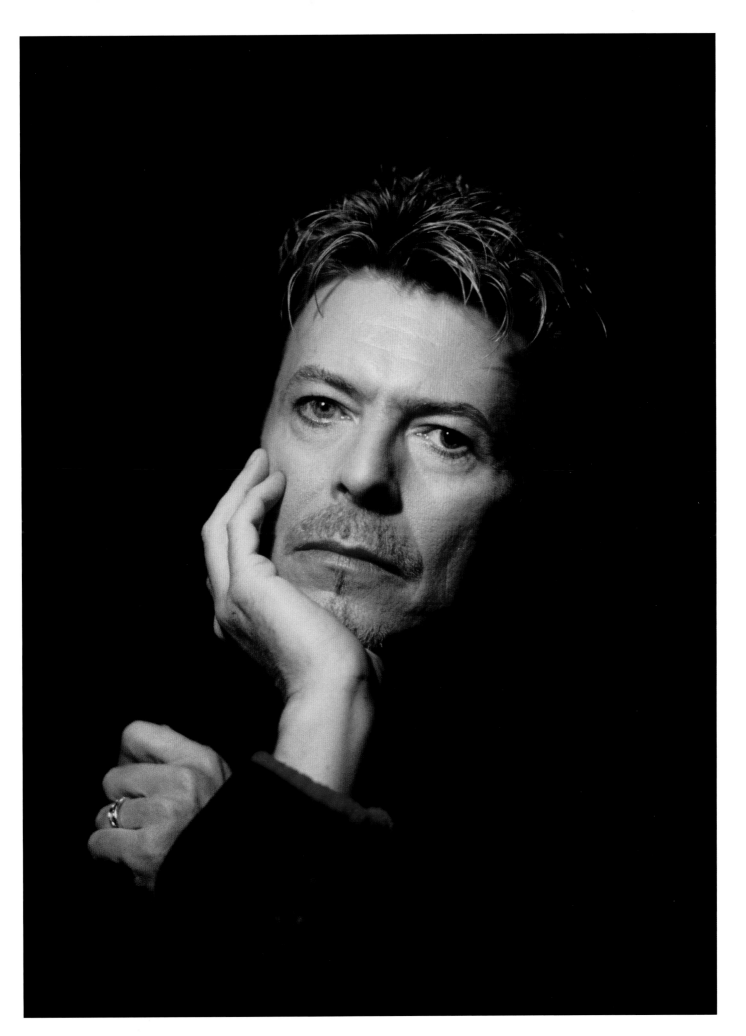

She and three of her girlfriends went and were hanging there for an hour or two before we got there. They were all staked out in the hotel. When I went to meet David at the Carlyle, I was dressed appropriately for the environment. I didn't look anything like I had looked at the Continental that night when we first met – this was only about a week or two later – and Bowie didn't look anything like he looked the night that I met him.

I sat down at the bar, maybe four stools away from him, and I kept sort of looking at him, but I didn't want to keep looking at him – I was embarrassed, in case it was a total stranger. I didn't recognize him as Bowie and he didn't recognize me as Nile; so after about a half hour, I get up and I call his office and I say, "Damn, man, when is David getting to the bar?" and they say, "He's been there for more than a half hour", and I said "Oh my God, that's him!" So I walked over to the only Bowie-looking-like kinda guy there and it was David, and then he recognized it was me, and we started cracking up, and we were laughing. But then something extraordinary hit me, even though we were laughing and having a good time; to me it was beautiful because it showed his character, this showed the real human being that was inside that flesh.

It wouldn't have been racist for Bowie to have considered that the only black man in that bar had to be Nile Rodgers. That's not that weird. I mean, how many black people were at the Carlyle Hotel? But he didn't assume that, because I didn't look like the sort of club-kiddy guy that he saw with Billy Idol early in the morning at the Continental. I looked like a guy who should be at the bar. So after that whole thing happened, I went home and I thought, Wow, how cool is that? He didn't just assume... And that really touched my heart. He's got a brain. He thinks. Because I didn't look enough like Nile to him, he didn't assume. And he didn't look enough like Bowie to me. And I didn't assume. So we had a good laugh about that. At that point my girlfriend and her friends were all cracking up like, "Is this some strange rock-star ritual? Like, do you just sit down and sit near each other?" They thought it was like two spies meeting: "I only smoke Marlboro", "But the unfiltered type is...", like some stupid little code.

DAVID AND NILE AT THE FRANKIE CROCKER AWARDS – (1983)

This shot was taken three months before the release of Let's Dance, *David's most successful album. Nile co-produced both* Let's Dance *and* Black Tie, White Noise. *Some of Nile's friends – Luther Vandross and Carlos Alomar – had worked on* Young Americans, *so when Nile introduced himself at a New York night club in 1982 they immediately hit it off.*

He came to my apartment after that, and we were really heavily into the whole jazz thing. We didn't have an idea of the album at the beginning. When we met, David had just come off *Scary Monsters* and I had just come off of an album that was pretty scary – it wasn't going to sell, I *knew* it wasn't going to sell. We talked about jazz, and that's all we talked about: we never talked about Hendrix or Clapton, or Jeff Beck or anything like that, it was just jazz, jazz, jazz. We started going to different libraries and different repositories where they had lots of records, because in those days they were still on vinyl. We went to the Library for the Performing Arts at Lincoln Center; they had a nice collection there, so we sat and we listened to a lot of jazz.

We were really into big-band stuff. And – this is a guess on my part, this is not Bowie's words – I think the reason why he liked big bands was because he seemed to like the counter lines that would accompany a big band. So even if it was just a regular song, he loved all of the counterpoint notes. We went over to Jerry Wexler's house. Jerry Wexler was a partner in Atlantic Records. Jerry had a TV-theme-tune album lying on the turntable and David said, "Let's listen to this!" so we listened to *Peter Gunn* and it was the funniest thing. So when I did the chart for "Let's Dance" I remembered how much he was digging that when we were playing it, and I took a lick right from *Peter Gunn*. I could have sampled it, but I wrote out the part, and horns played it and I voiced it the same. I copied it! What the hell.

Most of our conversations were very light, because the jazz that we liked was so avant-garde and so weird we'd both crack up over the fact that we shared those tastes. But in one of the heavier moments, I sort of got a little bit offended and maybe a little pissed.

––––

DAVID BOWIE – THE MAN WHO FELL TO EARTH, DRAWING NUMBER 9 –
PETER HOWSON (1994)

Bowie became friends with Peter Howson after David bought two controversial paintings of Howson's depicting the Bosnian War in 1994 (including Croatians and Muslim *that The Imperial War Museum turned down due to it's brutal subject matter). This drawing comes from a sitting that year when Howson made 10 sketches at his London studio during a session in which Bowie appeared to fall asleep and fall off the 5-foot plinth he was sitting on.*

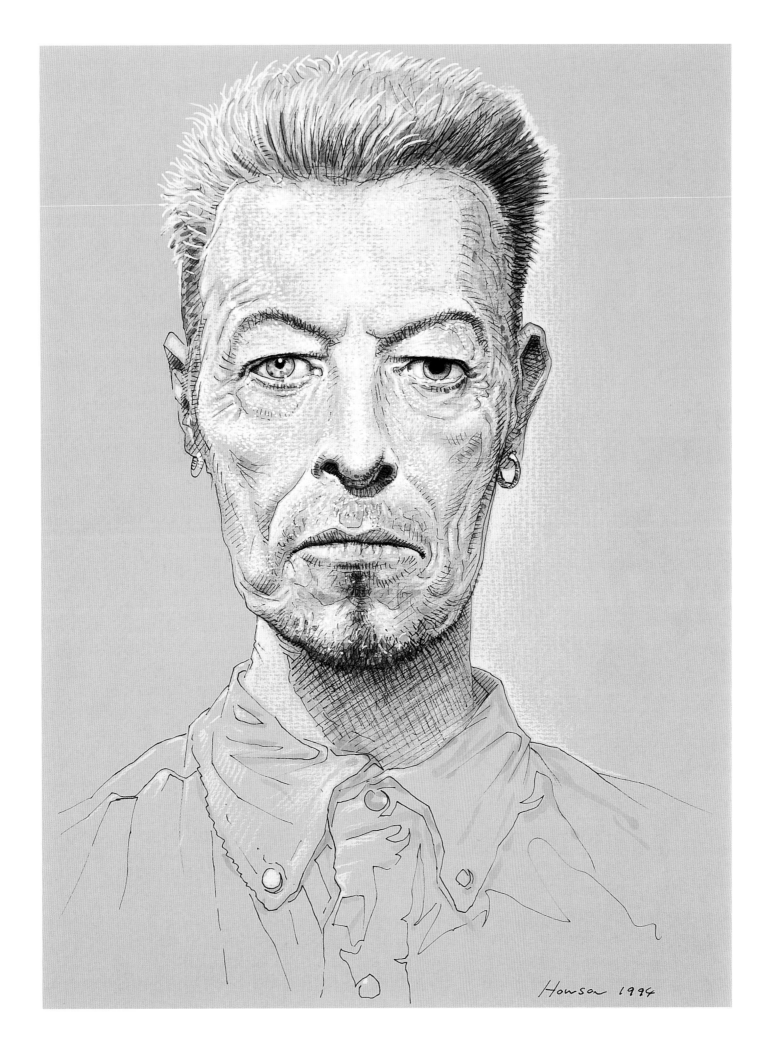

Howson 1994

He said to me, "Well, you know, Nile darling, I'd really like you to do what you do best." But I was always proud and very aware of all the stuff that I know how to do, but no one ever gets a chance to hear from me, because of the kind of jobs I get. I don't try and superimpose Rachmaninoff and Bach and Prokofiev on somebody like Pat Benatar. So I was hoping he understood how many different things I could do. So he said to me he'd like me to do what I did best, and I asked him what he thought that was, because, I was like, "You don't *know* what I do best."

He says, "You do hits."

I said, "What?"

He says, "You do hits. I'd like you to do a record of hits."

And for a minute I was upset, because I was coming from the whole "disco sucks" thing. I hadn't had a hit record in six albums, and this sounds weird but, until "disco sucks", and the Diana Ross album I worked on, every single record I did was a hit. It's how I started out. My first record was platinum, second record was platinum, every single record, so Bernard Edwards and I had gotten to the point where we would get a call from Atlantic Records and we'd say, "Oh, *another* gold record, or *another* platinum record...?" So I went from everything being successful to nothing.

No one called, no one cared. Whatever I tried to do, no one was interested. And I realized I was tagged with this scarlet letter of "Disco". It was like, wow, has anyone ever listened to a Chic album? I know you may hear "Le Freak" and think that's all we do, but listen to our albums, I don't mean this in an egotistical way, I'm really just trying to give you facts: I have played with great musicians all my life. I have never played with sucky bands. I don't believe in it. And not many guitar players could play the stuff that I play on the first couple of Chic records. Let 'em play "Savoir Faire". They don't even know their chord changes, they don't even understand tertiary harmony, for God's sakes; they learn chords, like a guy goes, "Hey, this is a D chord, hey, this is G chord, hey, this is E-minor chord," and that's what they do. That's what they play every time. That chord's a C.

That's not what I learned. I learned proper harmony and I learned to read music, and when I do a session I voice-lead on the guitar to complement the other players around me. I'm not trying to be, like, the star, I'm trying to be part of ensemble.

David asking for hits really threw me. Because he had just come off of *Scary Monsters*, an album that I liked quite a bit, but I respect artists who make records that they like. They don't have to be hits. I've certainly bought my share of "flops". Hell, I've made my fair share of flops. In fact, that's what I do: I make flops, and every now and then I get a hit. That's the truth. So when he told me that, I was taken aback, I was stunned, but the opportunity to work with Bowie...

I remember David coming to my apartment one day. He knocked at my door and he had his hands behind his back like this, and he says, "Now, darling, this is what I want my album to sound like." And it was a picture of Little Richard in a red suit getting into a red Cadillac and it was all monochromatic. Richard's hair was dyed kind of red. Suit red. Cadillac red. It was just red. And as soon as David showed me that picture I understood it like a perfect mathematic equation or a perfectly written sentence. A nano-second, and then I thought, Oh! He wants a record that sounds like it's from the future even if we release the record in 3020. Because that's what this Little Richard picture looks like. That's a 1960 Cadillac, but it looks like they'd just taken the photo that morning, right out in front of the building. And I knew that he wanted the record to be evergreen, but that's the last thing he wanted me to say. He wanted me to hear it from the way that that thing looked. It made all the sense in the world to me. In that moment, I describe myself as being like the Terminator. At that point there was no going back for me. I was focused, I knew the record we were going to make, and if it felt he was going off the rails, it was on me to be, "Er, David, no." I almost wanted to keep the picture of Little Richard in my pocket and say, "Dude, do you think that sounds like this?" You know? But I didn't have to. It was easier than that.

Half of the album's songs existed before we walked in that studio. He was allowing me to interpret music that already existed. So it's almost like taking a fully cooked fine

THE POWER STATION (1982)

*David, Stevie Ray Vaughan and Nile Rodgers during the "Let's Dance" recording sessions at
The Power Station, New York where Bowie had recorded his previous album* Scary Monsters.
*"Let's Dance" was the first song recorded for the album and it went on to become Bowie's
only transatlantic number one.*

meal, it's all beautiful, and then you say to the chef, "Hey, can you make something different out of this?" Had he not shown me the Little Richard picture, I might have made "China Girl" into some hardcore, trashy thing. Once he showed me that picture of this sleek, debonair, not-a-hair-out-of-place guy, though, to me that just telegraphed consistency, unity, precision, perfection.

———

No one knew this until recently, but I finally told the truth about the first time I ever heard Bowie... I was down in Miami Beach, gigging with different bands, when I met this girl who's a photographer at a club, like a Hawaiian joint. She was gorgeous, and she said, "There's a nude beach called Dania Beach and I'd like to make love with you and watch the sun rise and listen to my favourite artist." Cool. I mean, was I going to ponder this? "Well, you know, I've got things I have to do, my love, so, sorry..."

And I never told him, because by the time we met I'd already done Diana Ross and stuff. So my concept of Bowie was *insanely* romantic, and the fact that Carlos Alomar and Luther Vandross and Robin Clark were involved – all these people I've known all my life – basically, that was Chic, the people I made my first record with, you know, were on *Young Americans*. Wow. And now I get to be his partner? Are you kidding me? This is the best opportunity *ever*. *Let's Dance* was the Eighties version of *Young Americans* in some ways.

It always makes me feel uncomfortable to say stuff like this because a person would take it the wrong way, but let's try and look at it from my perspective. That record, I made. Period. End of story. Yes, David sang. Yes, he wrote songs. But here's what we did: we had a brand-new studio in Power Station, Studio C, and it had a really nice lounge; I made a record, we would walk in the lounge after we cut the track and he would listen, and he'd give a nod of approval. I never once had him say, "Do that song

again." If you look at all the years that have gone by, you never heard any outtakes from *Let's Dance*. We did it like a black record, and the way that black records were done in those days is that we didn't have studios locked out. We didn't have the budgets like rock 'n' roll bands had – our albums would cost $30,000 to make. So, David came in, we played the song. Boom. Right. Good. Great. Next one. Played that one. Good. Right. Next one. Right. Next one...

The only thing that we sort of went back and forth over was a song that we created in the studio. And I think that was "Ricochet". It was the very first time in my entire life that I did a recording session where I didn't have the charts written before we got there. He came up with this riff and I had to come up with the charts right there on the spot. I had to say, "OK, right, here's how it goes," because usually I like to sit at home and do a proper arrangement, but since it just happened right there, I had to do the charts on the spot. And I think it was Lenny Pickett or someone said a phrase I'd never heard in my life before, and I'd been making music for ever. He said, "Hey, Nile, why don't you just do head charts?" And I was like, "What the hell's a head chart?" I'm a hippy, so, to me, "head" is a person who does acid. Like a head chart would be, "Oh, wow, man, let's do head charts!" I didn't know what the hell he was talking about, because we were very organized: the school I come from, you come in, read the charts, do that, do the next song, read the charts...

So Bowie fell right into my world. He didn't know one other musician on that album other than me and Stevie Ray Vaughan. He'd never heard of Omar Hakim, who played

---

CENTURION – CAROLYN DJANOGLY (1999)

A smiling David shot in 1999 for portrait photographer Carolyn Djanogly's book Centurions. *The volume contained portraits of 100 people who had significantly influenced the social, political and cultural texture of 20th Century Britain.*

drums on the album. He's like, who's playing keyboards on my album, who's singing backing on my album, who are these guys? I can't tell you how amazing that makes me feel. A guy I *worship*, not just because of the way I first heard his music – yeah, the girl was awesome, the beach was awesome – but, man, I couldn't get "Suffragette City" out of my head. I was into that for weeks and weeks and weeks after. I had that album so memorized I would walk around the house singing it.

When he asked who the musicians were, I said, "These are some of the best musicians I know and I've had rock 'n' roll bands with all of them; they are the most frustrated guys in the world, because they love rock 'n' roll and they don't get a chance to play it. You're giving them the chance to play David Bowie? We're going to *kill* your shit. We are going to Kill. Your. Shit."

True story: when our other drummer, Tony Thompson, came in to play, the sound-pressure levels were so hardcore in the studio that the lights would dim every time he hit that snare. And this is The Power Station. Right? I was like, I'm glad I'm not standing in that room. A lot of anger and frustration came out – and it wasn't directed at David, it was anger directed at the industry; it was the fact that this is what we love, we could play this all day long, give us a chance. David Bowie gave us a chance. And we ripped it.

David showed 100 per cent trust. I felt this is exactly what David wanted. He said he wanted me to make hits. And how do I make hits? I'm the boss. I write the charts, I write the songs, I tell everyone what to do and they do it. There's no arguments, we all have fun, everyone who works with me has the time of their lives, and they just do what I say and they go. We're done.

And then he brings this guy Stevie Ray Vaughan, who none of us had ever heard of. Stevie saw the camaraderie that we all had. David was all by himself in a room, not because he was weird, just because he didn't know anybody; everyone would go in and talk to him after they'd played their parts... But Stevie saw that we were all friends, all the musicians were Nile's musicians, so Stevie Ray Vaughan did the coolest thing...

David effectively had to pay for this album himself – for one reason or another. Maybe he wanted a hit because of that. So to keep the cost down, David would buy our food in the morning. There was no sitting around with a bunch of girls all day and drinking. No way, we'd get there, record and leave. We didn't have a session blocked out for months at a time. None of that.

We made that record in 17 days from start to finish. So here's how our day would start: when we arrived at the studio we would order our lunch, so that when we took our break we could eat and then go right back to making the record, right? No down time.

Stevie knew this. So this is what he did – he didn't have to play one day, so he got on the phone and called some joint called Sam's BBQ in Austin, Texas – and had them send up this shipment of barbecue, and in a day or so it arrived. It was the most awesome barbecue ever, and Stevie Ray treated everybody to lunch, and the camaraderie was like, "Bro, you're in, come over here. Come on, you're part of the guys." And from that moment on he was part of the crew. I loved Stevie like a brother.

───

If ever there was a person who was not a racist, it was David Bowie. And it shocked him, the response that he was getting from people who he had admired, working with me.

I mean, these were people whom he thought of as big thinkers, great artists, cool people. Like, all of a sudden, now I'm the guy with the scarlet letter of Disco emblazoned in my chest. I'm that dude. And it almost felt like David felt he had to apologize for me. "No, no, no, no, no. He can actually transcribe Eric Dolphy's 'Out to Lunch!'." I'm like, "Nah. Dude. You don't have to prove it to them. You don't have to cover for me."

But no. He kept saying , "No no no. Nile can write out the chart to '17 West'."

"'17 West', what is that?" "Oh, that's one of those great Eric Dolphy songs..." "David, it's cool, man. We're making a rock 'n' rock record. It's fine."

And then the addition of Stevie Ray Vaughan. It was like he deliberately wanted to combine these disparate people from these backgrounds that don't match. Your bass player's Puerto Rican, named [Carmine] Rojas, your drummer's named Omar Hakim, your guitar player's named Nile Rodgers, named after a river in Africa... And then you've got Stevie Ray Vaughan coming up from Texas. That's your band. And it was killing. It was a killer band. We did everything in one take. Whipped right through that record.

When I saw that look on Stevie Ray Vaughan's face when he heard that track, "Let's Dance" and I heard him listening... I've been around brilliant schooled musicians, I was raised with geniuses; I saw this guy calculating where the space was: "Where do I speak in this record that is complete?" This record was already complete to Stevie. He's sitting there, like, grooving, "Where do I fit in? Man, this is incredible." And where'd he fit in? He plays one note. And, that's the note! That's the note, Stevie! "Thank you, I'm outta here. Now, let's get some Sam's barbecue."

Only Bowie would get this dude from Texas playing Albert King licks over this pop album that we were making. The incredibly fluid mind of David Bowie. I mean, nothing could have been more intelligent. When we searched around listening to all these records, the part I left out is that we listened to tons of rock 'n' roll iconography. We had everything from Mott the Hoople to Peanut Butter Conspiracy, from the hippiest hippy stuff to the Ventures. I mean, just every kind of rock 'n' roll record you could think of. We were at the Library for Performing Arts that's got everything, so we

————

HEATHEN – MARCUS KLINKO (2002)

This shot was taken by Marcus Klinko from the cover shoot for the album Heathen. *The eerie shot for the cover came about after the photographer had worked on the cover shoot of Iman's book* I am Iman. *David was impressed with his work and wanted the photographer to shoot the cover to his next album. Bowie brought along some Man Ray images that he wanted to reference and was keen for the shots to depict him as a blind man in a '40s suit. "Bowie knew exactly what poses and expressions to do in order to portray the character we discussed. He was very carefree and fun to shoot."*

could just look and chill and see what we wanted the album to sound like. I didn't know what we were doing actually. To me, we were just becoming friends and having fun and listening to records, which was OK with me.

———

Once David charged me with making a hit, I felt that a lot of his songs were lacking in ear candy at the top of the compositions. I explained to him that every song I've ever written starts with the chorus. And he says, "Really? Why? That's crazy. You build to the chorus." I said, "Yeah, if you're white you build to the chorus. I start with the chorus, because I know that every guy who's the promotion man who's going to get your record added at the radio station is going to go home with a pile of records under his arm that weekend, play it for his kids, and the one that his kids say is the record, that's the one he's going to get added next week. So, my records go, 'Do do do do do. We Are Family...' 'One. Two. Ahhhh. Freak Out!'" So I said, "David, I want the first words out of your mouth to be Let's Dance." "Ah, really? Usually I would build up..." "Ah, no, man, the first words. Like the first words go Freak Out. The first words go, We Are Family. The first words are Let's Dance."

Let's Dance turned out to be a hit. An 11-million-seller. Insane. He'd never sold anything like that. If you notice, all the interviews that he did subsequently, very few of them talked about me. I don't think David had anything against me; I think that he had survivor guilt or, like, you're so successful that you might be defined by this one record when your body of work is so vast. Me, on the other hand, I'm thinking, I can't wait to get to the next record! Let's do another record like *Let's Dance*. Let's sell 20 million records. I'm thinking, If that's how you look at me, and I've served your job well, sire, wouldn't you like me to go kill the next dragon? To me, it was weird that after all that fame and success, he didn't say, "Here's my boy Nile, the guy I told to do this." Instead, it was always, "Here's my boy Eno," which got a little tiresome, as much as I like Brian.

The dominoes fell at that point. I went from six flops in a row to back on the charts. INXS was next. "Original Sin" was one of their biggest hits. The next four or five records I did, became the biggest records of each of those artists' lives. So, the 11-million Bowie-seller. When I did "The Reflex", Duran Duran's record was already done. So they said, "Nile, would you do a remix?" And I said, "I don't do remixes, I'm a composer, a producer..." Then I realized, I just did that with Bowie. I mean, "China Girl" already existed. "Cat People" already existed. "Metro" already existed. OK, yeah. I can recook the cooked meal. And I told Duran Duran, I'm not a remixer, but I'm going to do the record the way I would have done it if you'd called me in the first place. And that's the biggest single of their lives. And then, Madonna's *Like A Virgin*. 25 million? Woah. Are you kidding?

So years went by and I was getting an award one night. And, man, this shows you the David Bowie that I so, so love. This is the guy who was sitting at the bar that day. So, he comes up on stage to give me the award, and he says something to the effect of "Ladies and gentlemen, I am truly honoured to give this award to Nile Rodgers, the *only* man who can get me to start a song with a chorus." It was amazing.

Stephen Finer

London-based artist Stephen Finer's distinctive paintings can be found in public collections from the National Portrait Gallery, London to the Los Angeles County Museum of Art. His portrait of Iman and David Bowie (1995) featured in the National Portrait Gallery's 2000 exhibition, Painting the Century. *Other subjects painted by Finer include Yehudi Menuhin and Marlene Dietrich.*

I grew up in the same part of south London as David Bowie did; he went to college in Bromley and a few years later I went to art college there. At that time, there was what was then known as an Arts Lab run in Beckenham in which he was involved. Curiously enough, we didn't meet at that stage – there was a gap of a few years between us. And I very briefly sang in a Lindsay Kemp performance at the Purcell Room [on London's South Bank]. But that was a few years after Bowie had ceased working with him. So, there were these curious almost-connections, although, when we did meet, I never mentioned any of that to him, because it seemed such a back story.

It's become a cliché about David, but it's absolutely true – he was very alert to lots of things; not just in music but also in art. He knew of my work before we even met. My portrait of Marlene Dietrich was on loan to the National Portrait Gallery (NPG) in London. He, of course, had been in her last movie, *Just a Gigolo*, and he'd seen the painting at the NPG. I knew of his interest in my work, and we bumped into each other.

DAVID BOWIE – STEPHEN FINER (1994)
*London-based artist Stephen Finer did several portraits of both David and Iman.
His process involves accumulating the paint over many hours reworking it until he has
the image that corresponds to his experience of that person. The original of this portrait
of Bowie hangs in the National Portrait Gallery, London.*

POLAROID – STEPHEN FINER (1994)

A polaroid of Bowie in front of his portrait (on his left).

Just as many years earlier I'd bumped into Marlene Dietrich – but that's another story.

When he and I met, he knew of my work and was interested in me painting him and Iman. He said, "I like your paintings very much. I'll certainly be in touch. Shall we go somewhere and have coffee?" I was meeting some cousins from the States and there wasn't the time to go for coffee, but I didn't explain all that, so he must have thought it was very strange me turning him down. Nonetheless, we hooked up later. We met while he and Iman were in London and the result is a number of paintings of them both.

The one the NPG bought was one that I understand he would have bought if they hadn't bought it first. In the end he owned several of my works. I hope it doesn't sound self-serving; he was just very alert and very responsive to painting in general and not just living painters.

Right until the end he was still responding, in his music, to the world he faced; even incorporating, you might say, his physical decline, and from it he went on inventing. And that's the characteristic people always mention about him.

There is a number of Polaroids from when I worked with him and I remember he asked if he could have one particular Polaroid because he wanted to do things with it. I don't know if he ever did. He said, "You know, you'll have copyright. I'm very hot on that with songs." It was a very professional approach. I've got a copy of it, but what he did with it, I don't know. I've never seen it surface.

What I learned about him – and a lot of people have said this – was how easy he was to be with. And also there was plenty of laughter. He had a very good sense of humour. In fact, there are other photographs, one particularly, of him really laughing. I can't now remember what the joke was, or what he was laughing at, but I think it was typical of him. For instance, when we bumped into each other – it was just in a commercial gallery – he was on his own and I guess it was typical of his personality that he said, very casually, shall we go and have coffee?

Interestingly, we didn't discuss art. Mine or anybody else's. Which I appreciated, because I didn't feel constrained in any way and there were no suggestions as to what direction I should take. I imagine that he was too sophisticated to interfere with what an artist might do or what the result might look like, or indeed cramp my style. I guess he felt that if an artist interested him he would just let them rip, if that's the right word. But certainly we didn't have any discussions about art in general, which can be quite a relief.

In a way, because my portraits are beyond the surface appearance of people, it is about presence and personality. And that's why sometimes when people have said to me, why don't you paint so-and-so? and name a well-known person, I don't; because if I hadn't met them, I would find lots of things missing. Although it's not a photographic end result, you can't know much even about skin texture. Another thing that I strongly did have a sense of after meeting him and Iman is scale. And that is something that if you know someone from photographic images, or stage or film, you can't always know. Especially famous stars from the past; I understand Gloria Swanson, for instance, was a very small woman, but you wouldn't know that on screen.

I'm not trying to make a point about someone or draw out something, because once the presence comes across or is felt by me, it translates itself eventually, by persistence, into a painting, an image. I'm not sure if that makes sense or if it sounds like art gobbledegook! Although there's no painting of him laughing, that was very much part of his person. Humour, the way his laugh sounds, you know. Very physical.

David, as we know, worked sometimes by cutting and pasting lyrics; presumably, part of that is that it comes up with some surprises, which is common to painting – at least my paintings. I want the end result to be a surprise to myself. Not really knowing where it came from or how I got there.

"IMAN AND DAVID BOWIE" RIGHT-HAND PANEL – STEPHEN FINER (2000)

This is the right-hand part (depicting David) of a diptych with Iman painted by Finer in 2000.

Although he didn't say very much, I do know that he liked the one you see on page 161, which is the one that the NPG bought. We never had that kind of conversation where he said, "I like the way you've brought out this or that..." Well, he didn't say it directly to me. It's very gratifying to see people responding to it now, saying, "I don't know much about art, but it seems to have captured him..." Which is very, very gratifying.

I saw him perform at Wembley, in 1995. He was very strong on the visual aspect of his shows. Of course, a lot of that came out in the exhibition [*David Bowie Is*]. Again, it's a hackneyed phrase but he was a visual person. A very visual person. Not just in his own work, but in terms of what he was like on stage.

He had so many personae, from being a teenager until his death. There was this sense of somebody constantly reinventing themselves musically, and that also went into his response to art. Other, older rock musicians, they either go on repeating, or they do versions of what they may have done before. He didn't do that. Even serious health upsets became part of the process and a way of husbanding his physical resources. And how he managed to get into the studio to do *The Next Day* without people knowing... that was a real achievement. After his marriage to Iman, and the birth of Lexi, that was another phase... He clearly altered his life, but he never dropped his musical ambitions.

When he released *Blackstar* on his birthday, I listened to it that day, not knowing the implications – it was Friday, and he died on the Sunday. Because of that time-zone [difference], I heard about it early in the morning, London time, and, the next thing, I just jumped out of bed. Very few people knew he had cancer, because of this heart-scare-problem thing, and at first I thought that would be why he'd died, but there we are. It was a real shock, as it was to so many other people.

Without reading between the lines, as people have done with hindsight – "Lazarus" and all the implications – there was something discrete, under the skin. Now we know it was even more poignant.

———

MARLENE DIETRICH ON STAGE – STEPHEN FINER (1997)

This painting of Dietrich was one of several by Finer including the one that Bowie had seen at the National Portrait Gallery, London that had so impressed him (see page 160).

Gail Ann Dorsey

After moving to London at the age of 22 to pursue a career as a musician, Gail Ann Dorsey collaborated with artists including Boy George and The Charlie Watts Big Band, and appeared on hit British TV show The Tube. *She moved to Woodstock, New York in 1994, and joined David Bowie's band as bass player and occasional vocalist starting on his* Outside *tour. She toured and recorded with him consistently over the following decade, and went on to play on 2013's* The Next Day.

It is not often, if ever, that someone enters your life who can change the very course and essence of your creative existence in a subtle yet deeply profound way... Change your idea of who you are, what you are capable of, alter the expansion of your perception of the world... Who you will become... All of those aspects and more were ignited and set into motion the moment I received a telephone call out of the blue from David Bowie in the spring of 1995.

That's how it happened for me. I later came to realize was anything but random or left to chance. There was perhaps a small element of uncertainty, but there was always confidence and plenty of faith, respect and a gentle yet persistent demand for your personal best from David. And never more have I wanted to reach the peak of my potential than when I was working in his presence and in service to his music and artistic vision. That is what I came to know about working with a true master of his craft, David Bowie.

PORTRAIT – FERGUS GREER (2001)

This portrait taken by Fergus Greer was donated to The National Portrait Gallery, London in 2004. In 2001, David and Iman's first child, Alexandria Zahra Jones, was born. That year, Bowie was also voted by readers of the UK's foremost music magazine NME *as the most influential artist of all time. He was in his adopted home of New York on September 11th and in the aftermath played an emotional set at The Concert for New York City.*

BOWIE AND HIS BASSIST, LONDON (2002)

*David and Gail are seen here performing at BBC's Maida Vale Studio in BBC Radio 2's
David Bowie – Live and Exclusive. The performance included a rare live outing for Bewlay
Brothers. The show was recorded ahead of the European leg of his Heathen tour.*

It was always a huge rush to get called in for whatever the next Bowie project was going to be. I was primarily his touring-and-performance bass player/vocalist, although I did play and sing on three studio albums, *Earthling,* in 1997, *Reality,* in 2003 and his next-to-last studio album, *The Next Day,* in 2013. I am also featured on a few live DVD and bonus-track recordings, but rehearsing, touring and being on stage was how I logged in most of my hours with David. Just about to turn 33 years old and in the absolute prime of my life (if I must say so myself!), I was recruited into a musician's dream fantasy. Even though I totally dug his music, and especially his amazing voice, I wasn't exactly a Bowie "fanatic" growing up. On some level, I have always upheld my commitment of maintaining a solo career for myself, as well as being quite happy and content in my role as a singing bass player for hire, but it never in a million years crossed my mind that I would be chosen to join the ranks of the outstanding musicians who were the alumni of one of the most prestigious and infamously kick-ass support bands in music history – "David Bowie's Band"!

———

It is truly difficult to adequately put into words what it feels like to be a part of Bowie's legacy. From 1995 until his passing, I was repeatedly bestowed the privilege of sharing a stage or a recording studio with the man, one of a chosen few who had the opportunity to witness his unique brilliance at work first hand. With an experience such as this, you begin to realize that any scepticism you may have had about an entity greater than our perceived human selves begins to dissolve. With Bowie, there was most certainly a divinity at work. I repeatedly witnessed his process of liquid expression and wondered how such consistently incredible ideas could be constantly incubating and flowing from one man's brain. Anyone around him could not help being stimulated by his energy, wowed by his intelligence and warmed by his keen sense of humour, something I personally adored the most. There was always a good period of time spent in laughter…

A willingness to play... Exploration was everywhere and everywhere was open to explore... Not unlike the bold curiosity and abandon of a child... Which, in essence, is one of the strongest traits of every great artist or scholar the world has ever known.

I never much saw David as a man of leisure as much as a man of purpose. He knew quite well how to have a good time and be light, but his life seemed to evolve around a relentless enthusiasm for work, for creating, for acquiring knowledge, for deconstructing and reconstructing... He observed and absorbed, and, then, somehow brilliantly always knew exactly the right moment to let go and leave it all to the universe, where the magic takes over. Working alongside such a luminous artist as Bowie was exhilarating, terrifying, enlightening, educational and at times intimidating and overwhelming, but no matter what task he put before his musicians and collaborators, it was always a welcome challenge; a chance for us to dig deeper, and another tremendously precious day on the job.

It's unfortunate but none the less common knowledge that being a female in the male-dominated music industry can be bitingly insensitive and unfair. For the most part, I have been extremely lucky throughout my career to dodge that bitter bullet. My wonderful male musician and bandleader colleagues have always treated me with the utmost respect and equality. I have been seen and judged solely on my abilities as a professional and capable musician. If I could do the job, it was my job.

It would be inaccurate to say I haven't experienced a few hurtful incidents of prejudice on my journey, but with David, and my boss before him, Roland Orzabal of Tears for Fears, gender was never more inconsequential. Both Bowie and Orzabal accepted and engaged me completely into their worlds and their process without bias, and with enthusiasm and love.

I consider the few years I spent working with Roland in Tears for Fears to have been an invaluable training ground for what was to come next. Roland was one of the first artists who pushed and encouraged me to raise my game to the next level, to step outside of my comfort zone and set my self-expression free. Bowie took the torch where Orzabal left off, and my education as a musician, as well as a "performer", kicked into an even higher gear.

Working with David gave me the sense of being an integral part of a highly efficient team of specialists out to create and design some bold, new landscape of sound and vision: no project like the one before, no established statement or familiar ground like the next to come... Thinking caps on! ...Leave any and all inhibitions or propensities for closed-mindedness at the door.... Be prepared for anything! Everyone had as unique and specific a role as David himself. All that was required was that you brought your own special set of skills to the music. His vision was always clear, and if it wasn't, it always revealed itself clearly to him somewhere in the process of becoming. You always felt you were "in good hands", and, indeed, we were.

———

It is no surprise that David became more private in what came to be the last decade or so of his life. In the time that I have known him, I always gathered that his personal life, and the virtue of secrecy as an essential tool in his artistic process, were paramount to him. In the past couple of decades, the integrity of our privacy has deteriorated at an alarmingly rapid pace. There is something to be said for being selective about what we share, when we share it and how we share it. It helps create a more authentic and valid form of meaning and connection that I feel we are unconsciously forgetting and letting slip away... Boundaries willingly surrendered and vanishing... In my observations of David and his creative process, I would venture to say that few artists have been more adept at recognizing and utilizing the power of mystery and anticipation to stimulate our senses and imaginations.

David once said to me, and I paraphrase, "Art is not always about what you add to create something, but knowing what to take away in order for the thing you're creating

DAVID AND GAIL, A REALITY TOUR – BRIAN RASIC (2003)

This was taken at Forum, Copenhagen on 7th August, 2003... the first night of A Reality tour.
Bowie had performed two warm-up gigs for BowieNet members both in the US and UK.
This would be his last tour. At concerts in Prague and ScheeBel (Germany) the following June,
David suffered what was initially diagnosed as a pinched nerve in his shoulder, but was later
identified as "an acutely blocked artery".

to reveal itself." His judgement was razor sharp, and his ability to manipulate and articulate through art and music, second nature. He was able to fully engage us on some far-out journey of self-discovery, all the while keeping us enamoured and playfully guessing, "Who is David Bowie, and what makes him tick?"... Waiting for the next instalment of... something... We never knew what, but we always knew it would move us, excite us, challenge us and touch us somehow... Deeply...

I have been blessed to work with so many incredible artists, musicians, vocalists, songwriters, producers and technicians in my now 30-year career, all of whom have their own unique and special gifts. All of us are unique, but there is, without question, only one David Bowie. His existence was a very special gift to everyone whose lives he touched in whatever capacity. We have lived during a time in history where so many great artists have been part of the soundtrack of our lives and cultures, and Bowie is undoubtedly one of the very greatest the world has ever known. We are blessed to carry him in our hearts and minds in whatever way we choose... That's the way he would have wanted it... Long live the individual who clearly sees his or her connection to all things... I am very grateful for having had my time under the wing of one of the great masters of the twentieth and twenty-first century, and for one of the greatest musical experiences of a lifetime. For David Robert Jones I will always hold a love and gratitude like no other... Unique.

Zachary Alford

Largely self-taught, drummer Zachary Alford started his career as a teenager, playing Manhattan nightclubs while still in high school. In addition to touring and recording extensively with David Bowie in the 1990s, Alford has played with Bruce Springsteen and the B-52s, among many others. He played on Bowie's 2013 album The Next Day, *and on demos for 2016's Blackstar.*

In 1995, David was ready to tour for his *Outside* album, so he called my friend Sterling Campbell, who had played drums on *Black Tie White Noise* a couple years earlier. David said, "OK, I want to put the band together and we're finally going to do the tour that I've been promising for the last two years. Thanks for waiting." And Sterling said, "I can't, because I just joined Soul Asylum, but call my friend Zach."

Sterling and I were at junior high school together and basically learned to play drums side by side. He knew that I had the experience; I'd just done the Bruce Springsteen tour. David didn't want to go through an audition process, he was ready to go – he pretty much had the whole band ready – so I just walked right in, no audition. And it worked out.

Initially they sent me the album when I happened to be doing a recording session for an artist on Atlantic in Bearsville Studios, Woodstock, New York. In between

---

BOWIENET POSTER – REX RAY (1998)

Rex Ray was an innovative graphic designer who'd worked on a few posters for the Outside *and* Earthling *tours. They struck up a relationship when Ray asked him to sign some of his posters. This image was one of his first Bowie commissions for the launch of BowieNet and shows a collage of Bowie's different personae throughout his career. A version was later used on the 2002 compilation* The Best of Bowie. *Following this, David asked the artist to design the* Hours... *(1999) and* Reality *(2003) album covers.*

50TH CELEBRATIONS – KEVIN MAZUR (1997)

Zachary with Foo Fighters' Dave Grohl and original Foos drummer William Goldsmith backstage at Bowie's 50th Birthday celebration at Madison Square Garden on 9th January, 1997.

takes with that group I would tell the engineer to put this cassette on so I could play to it; so I learned the *Outside* material that way. Then, a couple of weeks later, when it was time to do band rehearsals, I walked in. For Bowie, it was a mix of old and new faces: Gail Ann Dorsey, who was also only just starting; Reeves Gabrels, who had been in Tin Machine; Mike Garson, who had a very long history with David but had just rejoined his band after a long absence; the guy who was the musical director at the time, Peter Schwartz; and Carlos Alomar. There was no stress or anything; it was just a bunch of guys rehearsing.

Then we went to the rehearsal studio SIR and David was there, and that was the first time I'd ever seen him. I was in a big room behind the drum set and he walks in, says "Hi" to everyone; when he gets to me he looks at me and says hello, and I'm looking at him and I just suddenly felt starstruck. I had already toured the world with Bruce Springsteen; I'd recorded with Billy Joel. But this was the first time I actually had to avert my eyes.

With other people you can make a judgement on what they're going to be like, but with David, he had so many personae, which were so out there, that you just didn't know what you were looking at. But he was super nice and way more down to earth and just, you know, chummy, than I would have expected. So that also was a surprise. Then very quickly we just got to work. And he was a really, really great guy to work with: very easy and all about keeping things interesting. He wasn't stuck in his own mind. He knew how to ensure that everyone had what they needed and was comfortable. And that was important to him, I think. He liked to work in a comfortable environment.

He was the kind of artist who trusted in everyone around him. But also, he didn't obsess on all the little parts. In fact, we were changing the arrangements of all his old songs: he wanted them to sound more industrial, because we were touring with Nine Inch Nails, and also, even at that stage in his career, he never looked back. He wasn't one to get caught up on a particular detail of a song. So, as long as you got through the song, he was pretty much happy. It was also in a kind of rock 'n' roll spirit.

———

Touring with Nine Inch Nails kicked our ass. And it was a great thing. I hadn't really listened to their music before that; the only thing I probably knew was "Head Like a Hole", from seeing it on TV. Gail was also more or less unfamiliar with their work. But we all kind of fell in love with the music, and so that was cool. And then there was the challenge. The challenge of "OK, we've got to come out here and tear it up. We've got to follow 'that'." David was just confident that we'd deliver. The hard part was that we were still a new band. We hadn't really gelled. We hadn't gotten our stride. And here we were coming out and having to put everything together right after Nine Inch Nails.

We were playing the *Outside* album and a bunch of stuff from his back catalogue, with the exclusion of anything off *Let's Dance* and most of his other hits. So it was going to be difficult because we were also getting to know the material, and it was difficult material. In the sense that there wasn't a built-in love factor for it yet from the audience. We did well, though, and we were getting better as the tour went along, and by the end of that leg we were really firing on all cylinders; we'd found our groove.

David was definitely really enjoying himself – I think he'd got tired of reproducing the formula in the Eighties, and then in the Nineties he'd done his greatest-hits tour, *Sound+Vision*, so I think he actually enjoyed himself more throwing a curve ball and then watching it having to make its way through and win over the audience. I think that's what our job was: to win over the audience with the new album and just play our hearts out; David was going to be David, which was always fantastic. It wasn't going to reach a mainstream audience, but a lot of the fans were really into it.

Looking back, it was interesting because I didn't *want* to do these industrial versions of his old songs. Because I loved them. I was struck by what I perceived as insecurity. I thought, Why is he trying to gear so much to this audience, when each song stands on its own, just as it is? But it's a funny thing, because later Garson said to me that he really enjoyed playing those other versions. Essentially, we were never going to be the original version, so in a sense he felt like he was in a covers band somewhere when they were doing it exactly like the record. And there we were creating a new version of it. And I think some fans did come round to it and say, OK, I can kind of appreciate what he was doing with those – they're unique.

We'd been on the road for a year, so we had already built up a vibe, doing songs from *Outside*, plus looped versions of "Breaking Glass", "Aladdin Sane" and "Lust for Life"; so when we went in to do *Earthling* in the studio, it was just business as usual in a lot of ways; more of the same. David wrote most of the stuff with Reeves and Mark Plati, so I wasn't involved in the writing of it. My time there was quick, which a lot of artists I talked to who worked with David seemed to echo. You hear all these records like *Station to Station* and you ask, "Oh, what was it like?" and they say, "Oh, I just came in and overdubbed; two days." And it's like, "Ok, yeah. I know what that's like." And so that's kinda how *Earthling* went. It wasn't two days, but we'd come in and do maybe a song or two a day; they were pretty much there – fleshed out – not even as demos but as songs that just needed drums. So the only thing was I just felt the pressure of having to come up with a drum part that was going to fit with these loops.

He had specifically wanted jungle to be one of the main inspirations for the record. I had never listened to jungle music before David asked me to listen to it. And he liked to work that way very often. I spoke to the late, great Dennis Davis, who we just lost, and he said, "You know what my favourite Bowie song is?" I said, "No," and he said, "'Ashes to Ashes'." And he said, when they did that, David had asked him to play a ska beat, and he said, "I didn't even know what ska was." You listen to it and it doesn't sound anything like ska. "Ashes to Ashes" is just "Ashes to Ashes". Same with *Earthling*, we didn't know what jungle was, and he capitalized on that, so it became some mutant form – of course David could have gotten a jungle DJ if he'd really wanted a jungle album. So I had to basically, just off the top of my head, come up with whatever was going to be on that record. It was a lot of fun, though, and I was pretty much happy with what I did.

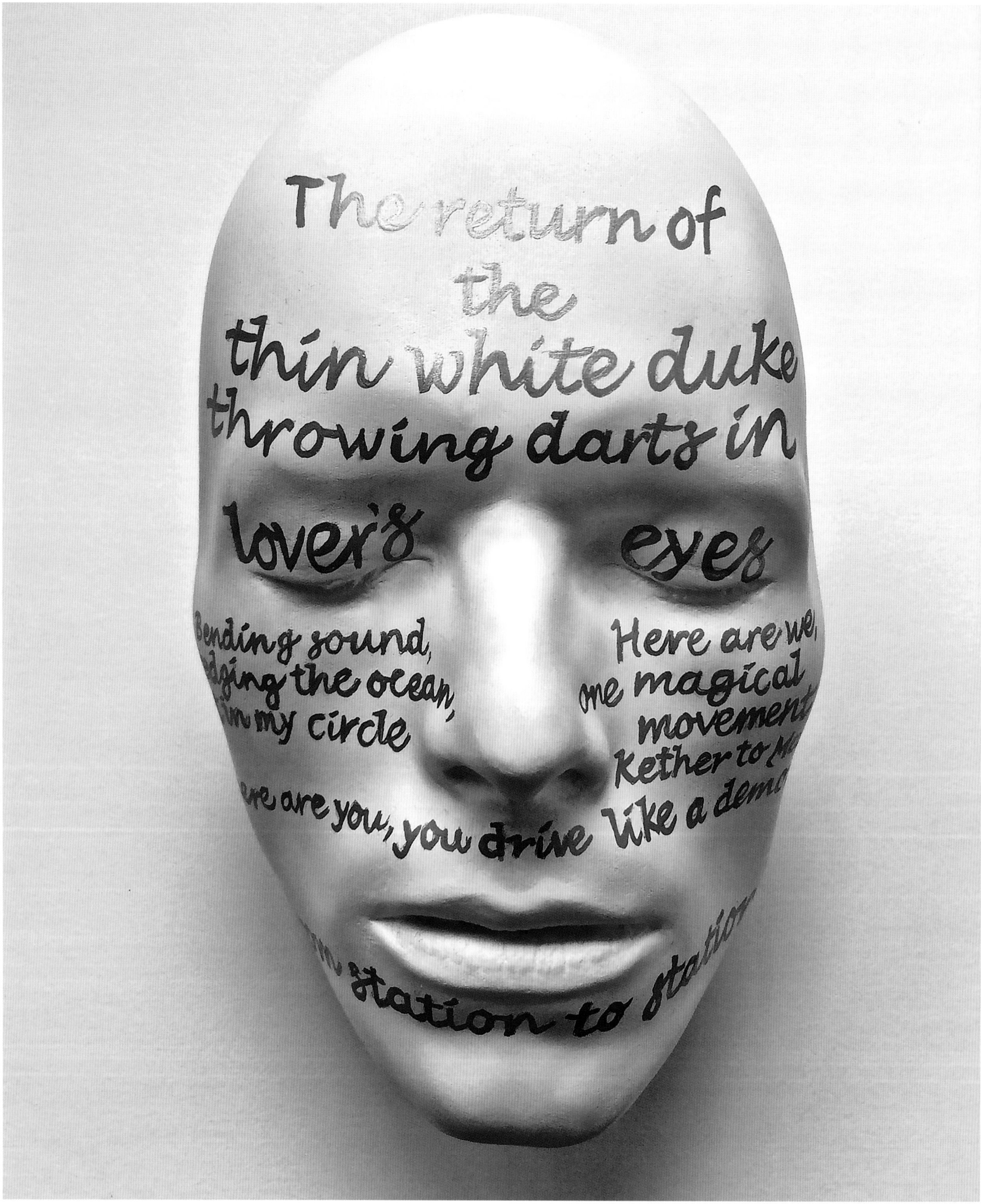
The return of
the
thin white duke
throwing darts in
lover's eyes
Bending sound,
dging the ocean,
m my circle
Here are we,
one magical
movement
Kether to
are are you, you drive like a demo
station to station

By that point we were also just really comfortable hanging out together. Particularly Mike and I. We had so much fun eating our way across the world, basically. That's how we looked at it. At the same time, it's funny because it's kind of a blur.

Then that was it working with David until *The Next Day*. We stayed in email contact; I was always surprised every time I got a response back, just, "Wow, he actually had time to read that." It was really casual. I'd hear from him on holidays, or on my birthday, or he'd recommend a book for me to read or a show to watch because it'd made him think of me. It was always just that casual kind of thing. Never work-related. Until *The Next Day*, which we recorded entirely in secret, when it had been years since his last album.

———

To me, *The Next Day* said he didn't buy into the media ethos that you have to put yourself out there all the time. It says, "No. Because of the internet, I can just release it." To be fair, not anyone could do that. But because he was David Bowie he didn't have to advertise himself.

You know, rock 'n' roll has a lot of clichés and stereotypes associated with it and I was never drawn to rock 'n' roll for those reason. Not for the fashion or for the lifestyle. I just loved playing music. And I think David was also more interested in that. I mean, he'd done everything else already anyway, so it was really just about the music at this point.

Recording the next day was really fun. It was a very professional environment, but we still spent a lot of time just chatting, telling jokes, looking at funny videos online…

———

WHITE MAGIC – MARK WARDEL (2014)
One of a series of life mask sculptures by artist Mark Wardel made from acrylic and enamel paint on a plaster cast. The cast itself was taken from an original taken in the mid-'70s to promote the film The Man Who Fell to Earth. *Bowie himself bought a set of six of Wardel's masks in 2015. The lyrics on the mask are from the song "Station to Station."*

And because we were able to capture the songs relatively quickly, there was time for that. It wasn't like these stories you hear where people are torturing themselves in the studio. David never did that. He wouldn't belabour a song. If it wasn't sounding the way he wanted in the first two or three takes he'd just move on to another song, and say, "We'll come back to that one." He just liked to keep a flow going.

David liked things when they were kind of thrown together just more organically. He liked to do a cool stage show, but he didn't like to go over the top. He wasn't into having tons of video screens and the latest lights. He wanted good stuff, but he wanted it to look more like something that was man-made.

I really wanted to redo one of the tracks on *Earthling*. I was losing sleep over it. It was the mix of "Dead Man Walking". The part of my drum track they decided to use, I just really felt terrible about. And he said, y'know, when you buy a Persian rug there's very often one part of the rug that is purposefully done like a mistake and that's to prove that a human did it.

———

During the first couple of weeks working on *The Next Day*, during the first round, at the end he asked, "Would you be up for doing some promo shows?" I said, "Yeah!" But then I remember hearing that sometimes he would say, "Oh, this would be a great track to do live," and then he'd follow up by saying, "But I'm never playing live again." So, you didn't really know what to think.

By then he had a daughter whom he very much wanted to spend lots of time with and he moved out of his place, the Essex House [on Central Park, South], and he was just fine in his life. But that was just the part I saw. After his death, so much information came out: interviews and articles and stories about different periods of his life. We learned how active he actually was even in the last few years. He was non-stop, so you feel like the David you knew was just the little piece of David he showed you.

He was so damn smart. I remember thinking on the *Outside* tour that this guy could walk into any college and give a lecture on a number of subjects – art history, Eastern European politics, or whatever. He was so knowledgeable, so well read. And on top of that, he had an incredibly analytical brain that could immediately process information. I can't think of any other pop artist that I could even have put in the same room with him as far as being such an intellectual powerhouse. And he channeled that into his art. He said, "I was never a rock star." He just wanted to use rock as a medium to communicate.

———

There were so many possibilities open to David and he was always considering all of them. I can't think of another artist who so wilfully just followed his whims and threw away what could be a successful formula. To get rid of Ziggy, to turn around and suddenly do ambient music, to then do pop music, and then to go back again and do avant-garde experimental music. He just didn't care if people were going to follow him. And he did things that would almost be the biggest turn-off you could imagine.

I remember when I heard the vocals for "How Does the Grass Grow?" from *The Next Day*. Based on the music I assumed he was going to sing something incredibly beautiful there. Instead he's going "NER NER NER NER." Like, man! It took me so long to get my head around it.

Now, I don't hear it that way anymore. I hear it as a truly unique-sounding vocal part. But at the time I was like, How can he have the balls to sing that? But he knew what the rest of us didn't know.

He never did what you thought he was going to do. And so if he was playing acoustic guitar for a take, I didn't know if he was going to keep it, or if he was going to overdub it. I had no idea what the finished tracks were going to sound like. There's this song called

"You Feel So Lonely You Could Die" and I'm dead sure, listening to it now, that that's the original acoustic part that we tracked with when we recorded it. We all played together, and he kept it. And thank God, because there's so much of him in there. And I think that's why he didn't like to do a lot of takes of songs, because he wanted to capture the honesty of those first performances. I've heard it called controlled chaos by certain people analyzing David's process, but I think it's actually more about honesty. He puts you in a situation where you're not exactly sure what to do and you do the most honest thing in that moment.

EARTHLINGS – KEVIN MAZUR (1996)

David with Zachary and the band at the 1996 VH1 Fashion Awards, Madison Square Garden, New York. From left to right: Zachary Alford, Reeves Gabrels, David (in his Earthling coat designed by Alexander McQueen), Gail Ann Dorsey and Mike Garson.

Cyndi Lauper

Hitmaking singer–songwriter Cyndi Lauper became an international pop icon with her debut album, She's So Unusual, *in 1983. She's recently branched out with blues and country albums, and wrote music for the Broadway musical* Kinky Boots. *In 2016, she took part in an all-star tribute to David Bowie at Carnegie Hall, New York City.*

Corporate people who don't understand performance art – the suits – would say, "Your image is so big, I can't hear you sing." That's why we all looked to Bowie, because he was one of the first performance artists and he didn't give a rat's ass; he didn't say, "Oh, I think I won't dress up this time." You know, he just fucking looked at the image and the sound, and put them together. And what he did was always really artistic, even in his appearance.

I heard Boy George talking once, too, saying when he first saw Bowie he looked at him and thought, Oh, oh, there's somebody else like me. That's why, when I met Lady Gaga, I just wanted to tell her: don't ever listen to what they tell you. I did, and I got plainer and plainer and plainer, and once I looked at myself in the mirror and said, "Who the fuck are you? Who are you?!"

I first heard David Bowie when I had left New York and I was going to Canada. I was going to go to Algonquin Provincial Park and do a tree study, just me and my dog.

SILVER KABUKI – MARK WARDEL (2015)

A painting (oil on canvas) depicting a silver kabuki mask with a "third eye" reminiscent of the glitter circle David wore on his forehead during his Ziggy shows of 1973.

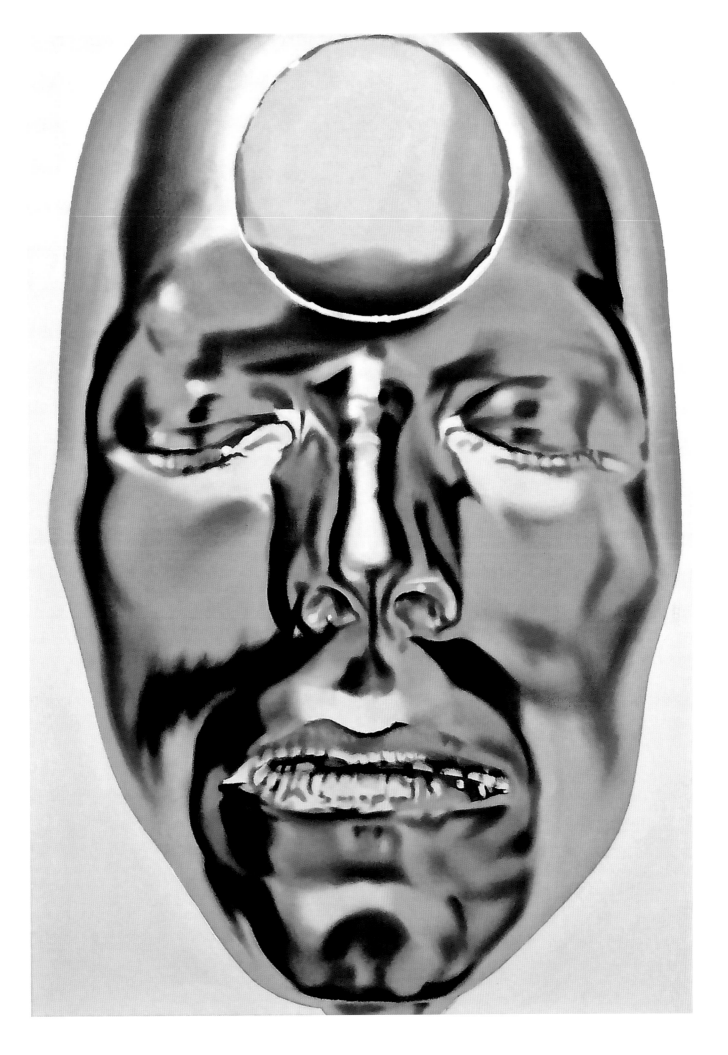

I was staying in Utah and started to become friends with all kinds of people, and there was this one kid who was always on the street singing David Bowie songs, and that was the first time I heard of David Bowie.

It wasn't until I got back from New York and then I went to college that I actually saw the *Hunky Dory* album and then became enamoured with his sound, what he was saying and what he looked like. I was in a band in 1974; at that time it was a cover band. We opened for Wayne County and then we opened for her again when she was Jayne County, after the transition. It was the glam-rock era, we played the Coventry Lounge, and there was a lot of gender fluidity, and then I started to listen more to Bowie. But at that point he did *Young Americans*, which turned your head again.

I'd listen to the background parts of "Young Americans", because I was a background singer, I had it in my mind that I was gonna be like Merry Clayton. I kept falling in the band – the platform shoes, my ankles were small and I couldn't dance and sing like that, and I would fall. And then the only manager that would manage us said: "I'll only manage you if you take the girl who sings good, that's dancing in the back and falls all the time; make her the lead singer." But when I was singing along to "Young Americans", I did the background. When I was driving home in the car with Richie, my boyfriend and the guitar player in my band (I was very much in love with him at the time), we'd listen to it. Then when "*Heroes*" came out – there was another heart stopper – we'd listen to every single thing on it, and we'd talk about it, and we'd listen to the whole album on the way back home.

No matter what he did, Bowie was first. If I was writing and got stuck, my friend would go: Bowie would cut all the lyrics up and move them around the page. And I thought, It's like artwork, like a collage, of course. And then you do it and you get unstuck and then you think, Wow, Bowie did that. He was just that kind of artist; he kinda led the way.

I met him a couple of times. I met him once when I was in the studio at the Hit Factory in New York City; I never said anything to him, and I kinda wished I

SUFFRAGETTE CITY (2016)

*Cyndi and Tony Visconti kick off the Carnegie Hall tribute with a rendition of
"Suffragette City."*

did. You know how it is when you're in the studio, you feel like you don't wanna really intrude. The next time I saw him was at one of Ingrid Sischy's parties.

I was such an asshole. I should have said something to him. I should have just said, "Listen, thank you." And much later when they said, "We're gonna do this tribute to Bowie at Carnegie Hall," I thought he would be there, and I would be able to show him how much he meant to me. We agreed to do it, and then as it was coming up, he died. I understand not wanting to die in the public eye.

He curated all his work, right up to the end; he knew exactly what he wanted to leave behind. You can only aspire to be that kind of artist, that what you leave behind is that important – and it is, it is important. You should never have to sing shit. You should always only sing the stuff that, when you're dead and gone, is gonna be there and live for ever.

Bowie didn't listen to other people. And, you know what, nobody should. If you're making your art, listen to the voice within; it will guide you. It will. I started out doing performance art. I got whittled down to fucking holding a flashlight because I thought, You don't need any of that stuff, you just stand and sing; you'll be fine. If you're a young artist, you should be who you are, and don't always listen to others just because you want to please; you don't want to be difficult: fuck it all; be fucking difficult. Your art is difficult. It's hard to be real. You don't have to fucking accommodate everybody; you're not a waitress, you're a fucking artist. Sometimes I forget and I wanna make everybody happy, but, in the end, if you're not happy with what you're doing, what the fuck are you doing?

Bowie was a real artist in that way. He grew. He didn't do any second verse same as the first. He took those left turns. He stayed real.

DAVID IN HUNGER CITY – TERRY O'NEILL (1974)

David at the rehearsals for the Diamond Dogs tour in LA, September, 1974. The set itself weighed 6 tons and had around 20,000 parts (later shows would have a more stripped-down design), which did cause the odd problem... a moving catwalk collapsed one night with David on it and on another the cherry picker got stuck over the crowd as he sang "Space Oddity" into a telephone receiver.

'An Icon in the Making'
Oil on wood. 2016
14ins x 17ins

Edward Bell

There was David, and there was Bowie.

One blue eye with flexible iris;
One green with an iris permanently dilated.

Schizophrenia was in the genes.

He could be cold and ruthless;
He could be charming, erudite, witty and
extremely good company.

David Bowie was undeniably a
multifaceted creative genius.

DAVID BOWIE – EDWARD BELL (2016)

This painting and poem are both by Edward Bell, who designed the iconic album artwork for Scary Monsters – which was based on a photo of David in the Pierrot costume shot by Brian Duffy, along with sleeve art from previous albums, whitewashed over as if "discarded". Bowie was so fond of the design that he commissioned Bell to do a similar portrait titled Glamour.

Robyn Hitchcock

Singer–songwriter Robyn Hitchcock broke through in the 1970s with his neo-psychedelic band the Soft Boys, immediately revealing his gift for vivid, oft-surreal lyrics. He began his critically acclaimed solo career in 1981, going on to release 20 solo albums. His collaborators have included R.E.M.'s Peter Buck and Led Zeppelin's John Paul Jones, and in 1998 he was the subject of a film by Jonathan Demme. He performed as part of the 2016 Carnegie Hall tribute to David Bowie.

People always eulogize the dead, if they're any good, anyway; Bowie was so fantastic. It was the start of the Sixties and there he was: very talented, very smart and very handsome. And very ambitious. You've got to have all four of those things in your sail in order to get somewhere, and also to have a bit of professional clustering, like the punks did. There were three or four punk bands around at the same time, so it all got going.

There was something about Bowie in his day that was very triumphalist. He was always about powering through and getting there and making your way – as he himself once said: "very Capricorn". "I will scale this lonely peak by myself." He was the Bob Dylan of the Seventies in terms of momentum – I think there's no question of that. I can remember people were looking around for the new Bob Dylan – it was going to be Bruce Springsteen or Elliott Murphy or Roy Harper; in a way it was Syd Barrett,

DAVID BOWIE – CHUCK CONNELLY (2016)
The acclaimed American artist painted this haunting portrait of a mid-'70s Bowie after his death as a tribute to a man he admired for his "sense of style". The painting was completed 33 years after the singer visited his New York studio.

but in terms of a sustained career and the phases that he went through, I'd say it was Bowie.

But Dylan was an angry guy, and Bowie didn't seem angry or nihilistic, or cynical in a kind of apathetic way. He seemed more amused: his music was more sort of about finding a place in your imagination where you could go and dress up. It's why he appealed to people growing up in the Seventies. Children dress up, they pretend to be things, and you just go straight from being a child to being a teenager, and there were all these things you could be. It was a vessel that people could reinvent themselves through.

———

I heard Bowie for the first time on a transistor radio that I owned, in an abandoned pigsty where I used to go and play. I was only 13 or 14. I think I'd just turned 14 so I probably wasn't dressing up any more, but I would go and sort of hang around there with my transistor radio, pretending I was on an album cover.

I'd reached that age where you took music with you – and I'd put the radio on the wall. It was probably around March, April '67, a chilly, British, bright, spring sunny day, and the song, "Love You till Tuesday" came on. I remember hearing that and thinking, That's smart; the bloke's probably listening to Dylan. I didn't want to rush out and buy it, but the name stuck – David Bowie – and then a couple of years later "Space Oddity" was a big hit, and then he disappeared again. I mean, he was around on the British circuit. I used to go to gigs, not as much as I wish I had now, but Bowie would be second or third on the bill with, like, Roy Harper – though I didn't actually see him. He was sort of like me at that time – a folky, solo bloke, so you'd sort of put him there, not enough to headline at a big show, but he'd be on the bill; he'd have his fans.

He had that aura of being theatrical and quite smart, somehow related to musicals – so it wasn't very cool, he wasn't very rock 'n' roll. He was smart, but it was a bit... off. It was sort of like, what's he doing here? He had the long hair – no one cut their hair between

1967 and 1974; they just carried on smoking the same joint and watching the revolution fail to happen, sinking into their headphones and getting ready for their first divorce or whatever. I could see it all happening; I was a bit younger. I was probably helping trigger those first divorces.

I had a bit of distance because I was only 14 in '67; I was 21 in '74, so I watched the whole thing not quite happen, if you like, and then Bowie gave this interview to *Melody Maker*, 22nd January, 1972, and he'd cut his hair and said he was bisexual... He'd sort of got a real jolt of energy. I hadn't even heard *Hunky Dory*, but you couldn't miss *Ziggy Stardust*. It was everywhere. And because he was sort of coming out, he was controversial; he was good with the publicity. By the middle of the year you had all these kids on council estates singing "Starman". He just simplified his message, and he cut his hair at a time when everybody was still very hairy and slow... Marc Bolan was a big part of it, but Bolan still looked like a hippy. Bowie was the next phase: he didn't look like a hippy; he was something else. Hippies could relate to it, but it involved removing quite a lot of facial hair and also moving over to the mullet...

———

Britain was always very style obsessed. London is like heating up a washbasin, it happens overnight; Britain's like a bath, you could do it in three hours; the United States is like a swimming pool, it takes a couple of months. So that's why punk never took off in the same way there. And Bowie was able to come in and absolutely crystallize things.

It wasn't like he was going against the times. There were all these other acts around that were quite clumpy. There was Mott the Hoople and Sweet. You'd get a lot of very hetero-blokes like Slade putting on lipstick and long hair and being pantomime, essentially... Glam was fun. It didn't take itself seriously.

The pop charts became very banal – they were very polarized between people who were valued artists that got introduced reverentially by Bob Harris on *Whistle Test*,

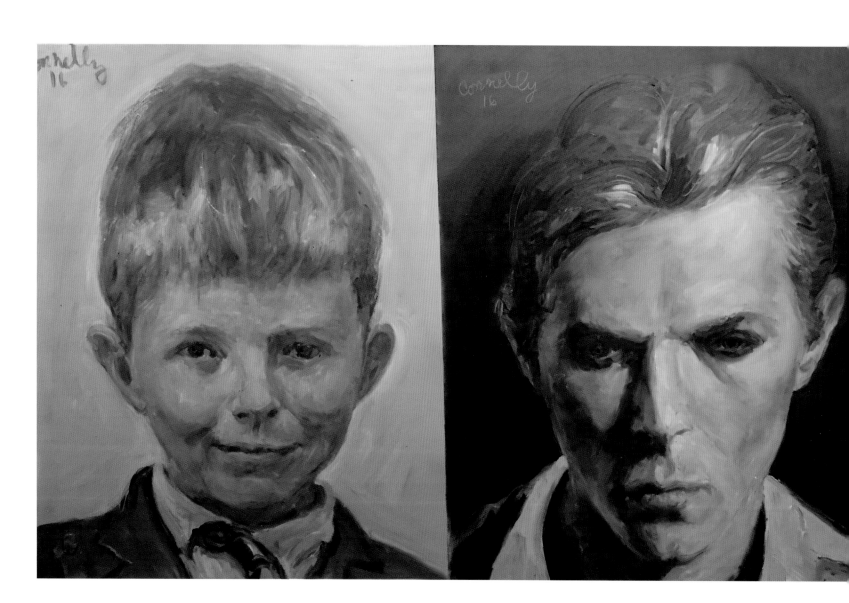

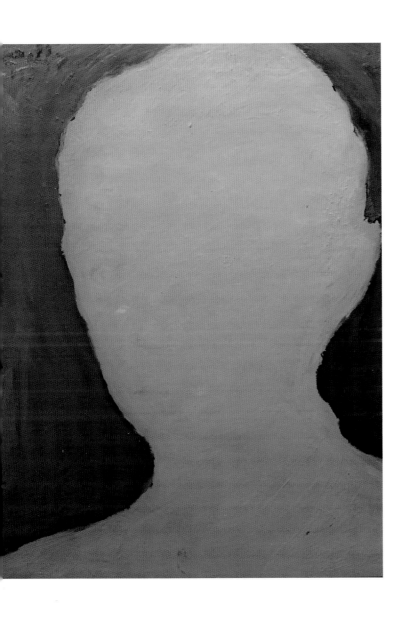

BOWIE TRIPTYCH – CHUCK CONNELLY (2016)
*Another work by Chuck Connelly depicting three images:
a six-year-old Bowie through to a "Blackstar" silhouette.*

singer–songwriters who seemed to take themselves painfully seriously, and then stuff like "Chirpy Chirpy Cheep Cheep", real bubblegum. There was a kind of chemical division between pop and rock that happened with '67. All those genius singles, like the Beach Boys' "Good Vibrations" and the Beatles. It all vanished for a few years, and then Bowie came along, Bolan came along, Slade came along, and you got these good, fun singles again.

Then Bowie got involved with Lou Reed, really helped relaunch Lou Reed: Reed was very cool because of the Velvet Underground, so people like me, who were Velvet Underground fans, listened to Bowie more seriously. People who were into the Velvet Underground were keen to see what Lou Reed was going to do, and Lou guested on a couple of Bowie's shows. Then Bowie revitalized Mott the Hoople, who were a great band who'd never had a hit. So you've got that whole Bowie–Ronson–Hoople–Reed thing, and then Iggy Pop; I didn't really know much about Iggy, except that he was very commercial. The Stooges really came into their own with punk. And at that point – which was another three of four years down the line – suddenly, that was Iggy's hour. Just like Lou Reed's was '72.

———

Bowie had good taste; he knew good music. I saw a thing he did about ten years ago in *Vanity Fair* on his favourite vinyl albums: he picked an Incredible String Band album. I loved them; I don't know if he was into Beefheart, but Syd Barrett and Lou Reed were very good. They were good songwriters in different ways. Barrett was always one-squeeze-of-the-tube-and-it-was-gone – that's why it's so good; he didn't dilute it, he didn't mix himself with turpentine like everybody else did; it was pure talent. Although that's maybe why he didn't last.

We covered the entire *Hunky Dory* album once: we used to do those albums in the pub, in London, in Clerkenwell, for Médecins Sans Frontières. I used to organize them

ROBYN HITCHCOCK – JEFF KRAVITZ (2016)

Robyn Hitchcock performs "Soul Love" at the Carnegie Hall tribute concerts in April, 2016. On news of his death he wrote this on his Facebook page:

Bowie was an old soul
He made the darkness fun
A star can go on shining
Long after it's gone

Love on ya, David x

with my ex-wife – there was a bunch of us, and we did the main Beatles albums, we did *Piper at the Gates of Dawn,* obviously, and we were wondering about Bowie. Obviously everyone had different ideas: Terry Edwards and I wanted to do *"Heroes";* someone else said we should do *Ziggy,* but the thing that got the most votes – although it didn't even get mine at the time – was *Hunky Dory.* But when we actually did it, I thought it was brilliant. You could say it was arguably the world's first indie album.

He hadn't become the Great God Bowie then, he was still this bloke, sitting in his flat, sitting in somebody's flat, with his Blend 37 coffee in front of him, cigarettes, popping out to the shops. And I thought, My God, this is absolutely it: it's a little bit of all sorts of things, held together by a personality that obviously loves music and other people's music, and you can hear it all in there: there's a song about the Velvets, there's a song about Dylan, there's his Crowley-isms, there's a lot of Dylan, there's a lot of Anthony Newley. Sometimes it's highly sophisticated music and sometimes he keeps it really simple.

I always say this: the deeper your roots, the broader your branches, which is why I think punk hasn't sustained, because it only drew on a few things. Bob Dylan and David Bowie and the Beatles listened to everything.

I mean, listening to Bowie doesn't make you a great songwriter but you get an awful lot to draw on, a broad palette. And Bowie knew all that stuff. You can see all his little homages, and name-checking Lennon or Jagger... Using all these people and then being the guy they want to be photographed with.

It's funny, if you sing some of my songs in a Bowie voice – probably the stuff I did in the Eighties more than anything else – you could make it sound Bowie-ish. He does a lot more major to minor than me. I think it's more that we listened to the same stuff. But he absolutely went for it: he had the ambition as well as the looks and the talent and everything. I'm kind of timid and quite snobbish. I'm more a guy who looks on from the side. I love an audience, and I could always do with a bit more money, but I never had that Rock God thing.

Also, it's nice if people recognize you, but it's not something you really want. I mean, you don't really want everybody to be looking at you. And that's like the curse of Bob Dylan. It's like some Greek myth. The Man Who Could Do So Much That Everybody Wouldn't Let Him Do Anything. *Life of Brian*'s almost about that, you know? "Fuck off." "How shall we fuck off, O Lord?" Bowie himself said it's not always good for an artist to be the centre of attention. And I'm sure he knew all about that.

What I like about him is that he seemed to deal with it all very graciously. He wasn't like Dylan or Lou Reed. He didn't seem to hate his fans for loving him. He'd get on stage and embrace it, yet not in a stupid way. He was able to mix high and low art, to do a real pop hit that also has avant-garde, almost unintelligible stuff. But it all works together.

———

I'm a huge Syd Barrett fan. I always thought *Piper At the Gates of Dawn* was a great mixture of pop and avant-garde, and, in a way, maybe Barrett couldn't handle the two opposite directions it was going in; certainly the Floyd audience couldn't. People liked the top twenty, they liked "See Emily Play", but they poured beer on them when they did "Interstellar Overdrive".

Because Bowie was much more of an orchestrator, or because he was a bit older when he made it, he was able to go and do all that. He'd give 'em the hits, but he'd also do these beautifully pretentious, doomy soundscapes with Eno and Fripp. He'd have Fripp's dissonance, but he'd apply it carefully. He'd have Eno and Fripp and Visconti, and Adrian Belew, his lead guitarist. He chose his co-stars well – like the Mike Garson piano solo on "Aladdin Sane". He didn't make it ear candy – he wasn't like McCartney; his instinct was not to please all the time. If he needed to, he could. He was able to come up with something like "Rebel Rebel" or "Jean Genie" and keep it down to three chords. I love Elvis Costello, but where someone like Elvis has to make things more complicated to keep himself interested, Bowie just thinks, Oh, OK, three chords, that's enough. Whatever he did, no one had done it before, although I don't think he could have happened without Bob Dylan.

Bowie kept that momentum up, album by album, so people could go: "Oh, what is he now? Oh, he's German doom! Oh, he's icy disco! Oh, he's Philly soul! Oh, he's rock 'n' roll!" I guess he had enough fans who were going to go out and buy it regardless, and it gave the journalists something to write about. I remember the reviews of *Low*... "Ziggy Stardust is dead and he's gone to hell!" The great Charles Shaar Murray wrote a whole page on him. He gave the journalists something to get into. In those days record reviews were longer; they could really get into "What's all this?".

Bowie developed, Dylan developed, the Beatles developed. They were times that allowed for development. There are other people like the Doors who sort of went in kind of at the top and it never went anywhere: that was all they did. Even Syd Barrett – it was perfectly formed and then it fell apart. I don't know whether I've developed or whether I've simply spiralled round my sort of three-trick pony that I am. You can't really assess your own work.

━━━━━

After *Let's Dance* there wasn't really anywhere for Bowie to go; he just made a bigger and bigger sound and sort of vanished into his own reverb. And he had enough fans that he could make records and they would always buy them. But they didn't matter. They weren't "bad," but if I hear them I think, That's nice, but I don't know what it is. It's like Bryan Ferry; they sort of reach a point, where maybe the world has taken your greatest hits and you're not going to have any more.

With his later records there was more of a narrative. Certainly with *Blackstar*, he seemed to have a sense that his time was nearly up. It feels he was very focused on it, and was in a very experimental place, trying to make something that hadn't been heard before. He was genuinely trying to come up with music that was not of a genre. It probably revitalized him.

I guess he just wanted to get everything done while he could. It's better than just waiting for the well-wishers to come and see you off and to bring in fresh grapes. I would like to go the same way. My father died: he was a writer; he had two scripts with him on the bed when he died. He wasn't writing much sense when he died because of all the morphine, but he still wanted to feel like he was working. Unless you feel that you've done everything, as an artist, you don't really retire. I suppose if you run out of inspiration then maybe you should, but if whatever you do is still getting to you, then there's no reason to stop. And if people don't need what you're doing, you still carry on producing it, just for the hell of it.

———

My partner, Emma, was listening to *Blackstar*, and she said, "It just sounds like he's saying goodbye." And I said, "God, I didn't think he was that bad. I'm sure he'll be around for another couple of years... I don't think he's off just yet." And she said, "It's that 'I Can't Give Everything Away', it's like he's signing off."

He's always been projecting his own absence. Right down to where Major Tom gets out of the capsule and never comes back. The idea is that you are going to go where nobody's been, and you're not going to come back. But the other subtext is that people are going to then follow you. It wasn't a sort of "I'm going where you can't find me", it's "and you will find me eventually, or you're welcome to come along." I think he was like an old soul, like he'd been around: he wasn't fresh in the way of John Lennon; he felt like somebody who had perhaps been through this life on multiple occasions.

STARMAN – SACHA WALDMAN (2002)

Shot for Entertainment Weekly *at the launch of* Heathen *in
June 2002. In the interview, David speaks of the sadness
of mortality and the realization that, at some point, you'll
have to let go of everything you love.*

*David died on 10th January, 2016, two days after his
69th birthday and the release of his 25th and final studio
album* Blackstar.

INDEX

213

217

Biographies

ZACHARY ALFORD

Zachary Alford toured with Bowie in the Nineties and recorded with him on 1997's Earthling *and 2013's* The Next Day. *He has also played drums for artists including Bruce Springsteen, Manic Street Preachers and the B-52s.*

CARLOS ALOMAR

Apart from Mike Garson, guitarist Alomar is the musician who worked most consistently with Bowie, including on Young Americans *(1975). He has performed as guitarist with a wide range of artists, from Chuck Berry, James Brown and Ben E. King to Bowie and Mick Jagger.*

TONI BASIL

A member of pioneering street dance group The Lockers, Toni Basil was choreographer of the Diamond Dogs *tour (1974) and* Glass Spider *tour (1987). She is also a singer-songwriter, actress and film director, and became known for her worldwide hit 'Mickey' (1982).*

DEREK BOSHIER

Derek Boshier came to prominence at the now famous 1964 The New Generation *show at Whitechapel Gallery. His work was brought to a wider audience through his work with The Clash and David Bowie. He worked on the cover for* Lodger *in collaboration with Duffy and Bowie, as well as other designs and portraits for the latter.*

GAIL ANN DORSEY

Working with David Bowie from 1995 until his death in 2016, Dorsey was the long-time bass player in Bowie's band, and also sang vocals – both lead and in duet with Bowie. She has worked with numerous artists including Bryan Ferry, Lenny Kravitz and Tears for Fears.

STEPHEN FINER

Stephen Finer's portrait of Bowie is in the National Portrait Gallery, London; he has also painted several portraits of Bowie with Iman one of which was in 'Painting the Century: 101 Portrait Masterpieces 1900–2000' at the National Portrait Gallery. Finer has also produced paintings of Yehudi Menuhin, Marlene Dietrich and Patrick Garland, among others.

MIKE GARSON

Author of Bowie's Piano Man, *Mike Garson worked with Bowie from* Aladdin Sane *(1973) to* Reality *(2003), becoming his most consistent collaborator. Despite training as a jazz pianist he has collaborated with a number of rock musicians, including Smashing Pumpkins and Nine Inch Nails.*

DANA GILLESPIE

Actor, singer and songwriter, Gillespie was a friend and former girlfriend of David Bowie. She provided backing vocals on the track 'It Ain't Easy' on Ziggy Stardust and the Spiders from Mars.

BIOGRAPHIES

DEBBIE HARRY & CHRIS STEIN

New-wave heroes and long-time acquaintances of David Bowie, Debbie Harry and Chris Stein toured with David Bowie and Iggy Pop in the late 1970s at Bowie's invitation.

ROBYN HITCHCOCK

Singer-songwriter, poet and artist, Robyn Hitchcock came to prominence in the 1970s with the band, The Soft Boys before going on to have a successful solo career. He performed at the David Bowie Tribute in New York in 2016.

CYNDI LAUPER

An internationally successful singer who broke through in the 1980s with her albums She's So Unusual *and* True Colours, *Cyndi Lauper performed as part of the David Bowie Tribute at Carnegie Hall in New York in April 2016.*

NILE RODGERS

Icon of disco and funk, Rodgers was lead guitarist and co-founder of Chic. He has worked as a producer and performer with many recording artists, including Diana Ross, Madonna and Pharrell Williams, and collaborated with David Bowie on Let's Dance *and* Black Tie, White Noise.

EARL SLICK

Slick replaced Mick Ronson as lead guitarist on the Diamond Dogs *tour in 1974 and continued to work with David Bowie over the next four decades. He has also performed with artists including John Lennon, Robert Smith and New York Dolls.*

GEORGE UNDERWOOD

Childhood friend of Bowie, and painter of numerous portraits of the icon. During a schoolboy dispute over a girl, Underwood punched Bowie in the eye – the injury is the reason his eyes appeared to be different colours

MARTYN WARE

Musician and composer Martyn Ware produces sound installations as a 'sonic muralist' and experiments with sound technology. He produced a data sonification of David Bowie's discography for David Bowie Is *at the V&A.*

PICTURE CREDITS

The Publisher would like to thank all those artists and their representatives who have made this book possible. Additional credits and acknowledgements are as follows.

9 Denis O'Regan/Getty Images; 14, 18 © George Underwood, georgeunderwood.com; 17 Cyrus Andrews/Michael Ochs Archives/Getty Images; 20, 22 David Wedgebury via Snap Galleries, London; 27 David Bebbington/Redferns/Getty Images; 30, 39 Ray Stevenson; 37 Dezo Hoffmann/Rex/Shutterstock; 40 Don Paulsen/Michael Ochs Archives/Getty Images; 45 Ralf Adlercreutz/Alamy; 49 Michael Stroud/Getty Images; 51 Michael Putland/Retna/Photoshot; 53 Ron Galella/Wire Image/Getty Images; 55 Brian Ward/IconicPix Music Archive; 56 Terry O'Neill/Getty Images; 61 Mick Rock © Mick Rock 1994, 2016; 65 Justin de Villeneuve/Iconic Images; 68 Richard Imrie/Camera Press; 71 Michael Ochs Archives/Getty Images; 73 Terry O'Neill/Iconic Images; 77 Sukita; 79 Robert Matheu/ Camera Press; 82 Brian Rasic/Getty Images; 89, 92 Duffy © Duffy Archive, duffyphotographer.com; 95, 98 Greg Gorman/Contour by Getty Images; 101 ABC Photo Archives © ABC/Getty Images; 102 Denis O'Regan/Getty Images; 105 David Plastik/IconicPix Music Archive; 108, 112 Chalkie Davies; 115 © Chris Stein; 117 Jeff Kravitz/FilmMagic for Michael Dorf Presents/Getty Images; 121 Christie's Images/Bridgeman Images; 123 Martyn Goddard/Rex/Shutterstock; 124 Clive Arrowsmith/Camera Press; 127 courtesy Martyn Ware; 131 © Derek Boshier, derekboshier.com; 134 Tony Evans/Getty Images; 136 Derry Moore; 141 Anton Corbijn/Contour by Getty Images; 143 Kevin Cummins/Getty Images; 145 Ebet Roberts/Redferns/Getty Images; 147 © Peter Howson, peterhowson.co.uk/photo Lighthouse Photography; 150 Chuck Pulin/Splash News; 152 Carolyn Djanogly/Camera Press; 157 Marcus Klinko; 161, 165, 167 Bridgeman Images © Stephen Finer, stephenfiner.com; 162 © Stephen Finer; 169 Fergus Greer; 170, 174 Brian Rasic/Getty Images; 177 © Rex Ray, courtesy Estate of Rex Ray; 178 Kevin Mazur/WireImage/Getty Images; 182, 189 © Mark Wardel, trademarkart.com; 187, 191 Kevin Mazur/WireImage/Getty Images; 193 Terry O'Neill/Getty Images; 194 © Edward Bell, courtesy Edward Bell and Peter Burden; 196, 200 © Chuck Connelly, chuckconnelly.net; 203 Jeff Kravitz/FilmMagic for Michael Dorf Presents/Getty Images; 208 Sacha Waldman/Photoshot.

SOURCES & ACKNOWLEDGEMENTS

Sources

These sites and works have served as references for the information in this book:

www.5years.com
www.bowiegoldenyears.com
www.bowielive.net
www.bowiewonderworld.com
www.dailymail.co.uk
www.davidbowie.com
www.derekboshier.com
www.georgeunderwood.com
www.illustrated-db-discography.nl
www.nme.com
www.rockpopgallery.typepad.com
www.showbiz411.com
www.snapgalleries.com
www.songfacts.com
www.telegraph.co.uk
www.ultimateclassicrock.com

Marsh, Geoffrey, *David Bowie Is*, London: V&A Publications, 2013

Rock, Mick and David Bowie, *Moonage Daydream*, London: Cassell Illustrated, 2005

Torcinovich, Matteo, *Outside the Lines*, London: Mitchell Beazley, 2016

p64
Sarah Phillips, "Justin de Villeneuve's best photograph: David Bowie and Twiggy"
www.theguardian.com
16 May 2012

P82
Richard Smith, "David Bowie final Glastonbury performance hailed as 'best ever moment' by founder Michael Eavis"
www.mirror.co.uk
11 January 2016

P94
"Exclusive Interview: Greg Gorman"
prophotoblog.ca
30 October 2016

P120
Details from:
"When the boat comes in"
www.scotsman.com
4 January 2016

"John Bellany Bowie Painting In RA Summer Exhibition"
www.davidbowie.com
4 July 2008

P127
Olivia Solon, "Data analysis of David Bowie's career turned into musical 'sonifications'"
www.wired.co.uk
19 April 2013

p137
Christopher Buckley, "David Bowie's House on the Island of Mustique"
www.architecturaldigest.com
31 August 1992

P145
Nile Rodgers, "David Bowie Changed My Life: Nile Rodgers Remembers His 'Let's Dance' Collaborator"
www.yahoo.com/music
11 January 2016

P146
"Peter Howson's wife to sell rare Bowie and Madonna work"
www.bbc.co.uk/news/
15 April 2013

P156
Marcus Klinko, "How we photographed David Bowie with wild wolves"
www.gq-magazine.co.uk
26 February 2016

p197
Kiri Blakeley, "One of America's greatest modern artists Chuck Connelly paints stunning portrait of David Bowie 33 years after the singer visited his New York art studio"
www.dailymail.co.uk/news/
16 January 2016

P203
Robyn Hitchcock, "Bowie was an old soul..." [Facebook post]
www.facebook.com/robynhitchcockofficial
11 January 2016

P208
Jeff Gordinier, "Inside David Bowie and Moby's out-of-this-world 2002 tour"
Entertainment Weekly, #656, 2002

Acknowledgements

The Publisher would like to thank Brian Hiatt and all the contributors, as well as Andrew Haydon, Patrick Cusse and Virginia Hearn for transcription work, and Trevor Davies for help writing captions and fact-checking.

An Hachette UK Company

www.hachette.co.uk

First published in Great Britain in 2016 by Cassell, a division of
Octopus Publishing Group Ltd
Carmelite House
50 Victoria Embankment
London EC4Y 0DZ
www.octopusbooks.co.uk
www.octopusbooksusa.com

All interviews by Brian Hiatt, except for pp 168-175 by Gail Ann Dorsey;
additional material by Trevor Davies

Distributed in the US by
Hachette Book Group
1290 Avenue of the Americas
4th and 5th Floors
New York, NY 10104

Distributed in Canada by
Canadian Manda Group
664 Annette St.
Toronto, Ontario, Canada M6S 2C8

ISBN 978-1-84403-927-2

A CIP catalogue record for this book is available from the British Library.

Printed and bound in China

3 5 7 9 10 8 6 4 2

Commissioning Editor: Hannah Knowles
Editor: Pollyanna Poulter
Creative Director: Jonathan Christie
Production Controller: Marina Maher
Picture Research Manager: Giulia Hetherington